IN THE ASIAN STYLE

A Design Sourcebook

IN THE ASIAN STYLE

A Design Sourcebook

FIONA DUNLOP

New Holland

Contents

Preface

For Westerners fuelled by the tales of Marco Polo or by romanticized etchings of later travellers, the word 'Orient' spelt exoticism and enchantment. It even echoed the word 'disoriented', which literally means losing the east and, by extension, losing one's sense of direction. Today, as the West looks increasingly eastwards for spiritual and stylistic nourishment, it is certainly worth reflecting on this. For Asians themselves, the concept of Orient is meaningless; they are already there! So in its place comes the geographical term 'Asia', to define a vast network of neighbouring countries, countries that, over the past two millennia, have antagonized and energized one another. Yet, however distinctive today's Asian cultures may be, there exists a common, albeit sinuous, thread: that of detail, refinement, ritual and sensuality. Add to this the techniques and forms, coupled with Western input, that have zigzagged across the region for centuries, and you have a richly complex approach to living.

Behind the historical design influences are two major civilizations: the great Indian subcontinent in the west and China in the east. Between them, today's political boundaries give us Nepal, Thailand, Myanmar, Cambodia, Vietnam, Laos, Malaysia, Singapore, Indonesia and, further east still, the Philippines, North and South Korea and, of course, Japan. Playing cultural games on this terrain are two concepts of perspective: the Indian, which covers the entire surface, and the Chinese, which gives value to space. This decorative aesthetic of extremes thus veers from the embodiment of *horror vacui*, in which surfaces are blanketed in breathtakingly intricate pattern, as in Thailand, to the monastic sobriety of Zen. The latter evolved from the Japanese perception of the world in tiny, brilliant cameos, each evanescent fragment being distilled into the bigger picture. This holistic approach inspired pioneering Western Modernists such as American architect Frank Lloyd Wright (1869–1959), notable for his 1920s 'organic' architecture, and continues in minimalist mode today.

My own contact with the East dates from early consciousness, as three generations of my mother's family spent most of their lives in China. From my cradle, I was more likely to focus on a pagoda bell than on a mobile and was later nourished by children's books on Chinese mythology rather than Winnie-the-Pooh. This evolved into a fascination for all things Eastern, which has been further stimulated by numerous trips for work and pleasure. Most recently, while looking at contemporary Asian houses for the purpose of this book, I realized just how much the basic tenets of these cultures remain, even in the guise of today's neo-modernist structures where computers are universally present.

With information so globally accessible and centuries of stylistic interchange already absorbed, East–West differences have become more subtle. In some cases, enlightened Westerners who have taken root in Asia have developed a passion for, and have imaginatively redefined, their adopted culture. In their turn, after decades of kowtowing to the modernist whims of the West, Asian architects such as Tadao Ando, Geoffrey Bawa, Lek Bunnag and William Lim have reintegrated their cultural identities without any shade of parody. In their wake, a new generation of architects is rapidly leaving its mark on the Asian landscape, whether in ingeniously restructured conservation houses in high-density cities or in rural settings where the scope is virtually limitless.

In order to convey this new synthesis, *In the Asian Style* shows the ambiguity of opposing forces at play: those of light and shade, outer and inner, textured and smooth, high colours and neutrals, complexity and purity, the noble and the humble, the traditional and the modern – the yin and the yang. For, ultimately, Asian cultures all seek that harmonious balance between form and material that encapsulates the essence. In the words of Lao Tse, the philosopher of Taoism: 'The reality of the cup is not the cup itself but the space within the cup.' Such an intuitive sense of beauty creates the perfection of a Balinese temple offering, the density of a Song dynasty porcelain glaze, the gentle curve of a Ming chair and the intricate weave of a hilltribe basket. Any one of these possesses an inner force. The masters of this genre, the Japanese, found a name for it: *wabi,* meaning 'respecting the essence of a material'.

Although this book cannot claim to be all-encompassing within such a wide-ranging field, I hope at least that the parameters outlined will prove as inspirational to people living in Asia as to Westerners with a yen for the East. In order to give a sense of continuity, I have chosen to concentrate on the warmer climes of Asia, where houses are designed to cope with heavy rains, high humidity, sunlight and constant heat. This is where spatial versatility reigns supreme – and results in some surprising juxtapositions. Although the contents of the book are broken down into structural treatments, exterior space, and specific areas for bathing, eating, sleeping and living, there exists

Previous page: A pair of 150-year-old stone statues from northern Bali reflect the spiritual side of contemporary Asian style at the Tugu Hotel, Bali.

Below: As much care, attention and time is put into preparing Balinese flower garlands as into any of the countless crafts of South-East Asia.

a constant interaction between them. This reflects the historical dynamics of the countries of Asia, where flux is the rule and Buddhist impermanence the underlying philosophy – the key to a specifically Asian approach to living.

Fretwork eaves edging the veranda of a Malay kampung house give definition to the foliage beyond.

   On my travels through Asia, I have looked as much at indigenous as contemporary architecture, sleeping in anything from bamboo stilt-houses to longhouses, yurts, palaces and cocooning hotels. What left lasting impressions were the indefinable pleasures of fluid space, sunlight filtered through a blind or reflections on surrounding water. More precise elements were the utter suitability of the veranda to the climate, the intelligence of natural ventilation or the use of decorative detail. I have been seduced, not just by examples of high art and architecture, but also by humble yet exquisite objects. Above all, I was struck by the ritualistic quality involved in manufacture and by that most intangible element of all: the time taken in any creation. Time taken for a Japanese tea-ceremony, time to weave a complex double-ikat, time to apply layer after layer of lacquer, time to re-thatch a palm-leaf roof, time to contemplate fleeting reflections on an expanse of still water. For Oriental time is something else: it is cyclical, not linear as in the West. That is Asian style, and our reorientation continues to follow.

FIONA DUNLOP

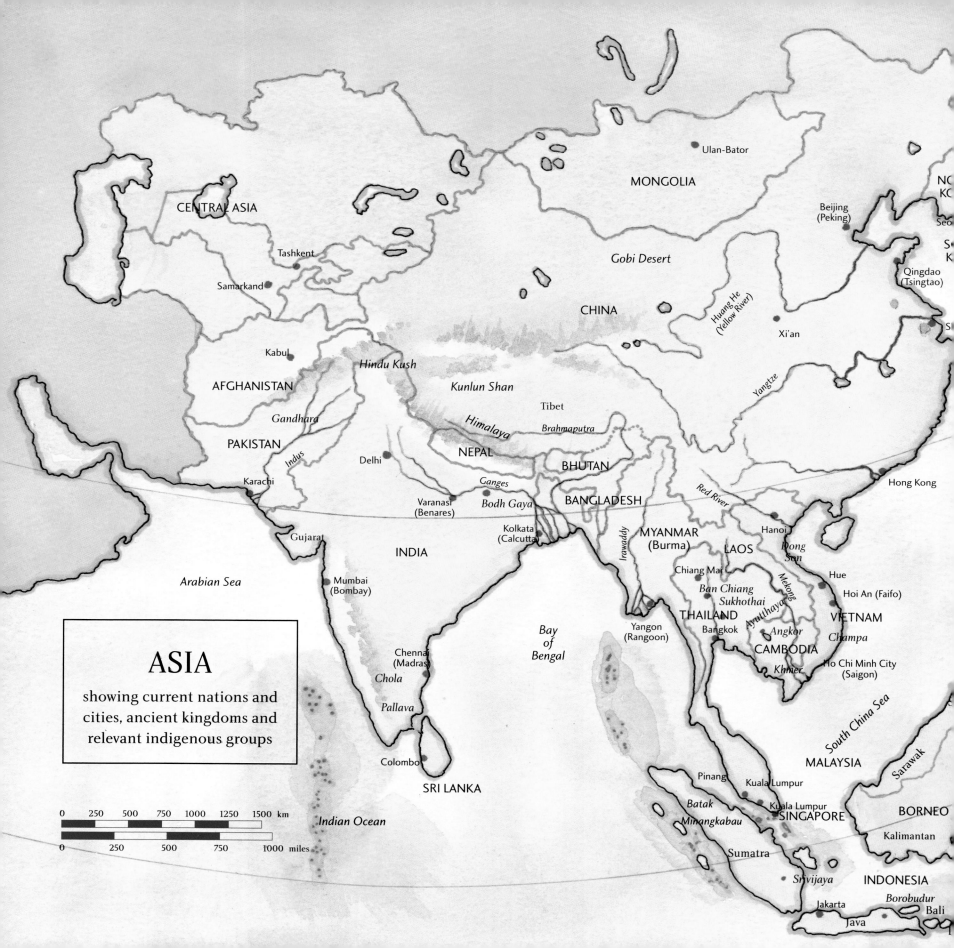

Ulan-Bator

MONGOLIA

CENTRAL ASIA

Tashkent

Samarkand

Gobi Desert

CHINA

Beijing
(Peking)

NO
KO

Seo

S
K

Qingdao
(Tsingtao)

S

Kabul

Hindu Kush

Kunlun Shan

*Huang He
(Yellow River)*

Xi'an

AFGHANISTAN

Gandhara

Tibet

Himalaya

Brahmaputra

Yangtze

PAKISTAN

Indus

Delhi

NEPAL

BHUTAN

Karachi

Ganges

Varanasi
(Benares)

Bodh Gaya

BANGLADESH

Red River

Hong Kong

Kolkata
(Calcutta)

Irrawaddy

MYANMAR
(Burma)

Hanoi

LAOS

*Dong
Son*

Gujarat

Arabian Sea

INDIA

Chiang Mai

Hue

Ban Chiang
Sukhothai

Hoi An (Faifo)

Mumbai
(Bombay)

THAILAND

Ayutthaya

VIETNAM

Bangkok

Mekong

Champa

Angkor

CAMBODIA

Yangon
(Rangoon)

Chennai
(Madras)

*Bay
of
Bengal*

Khmer

Ho Chi Minh City
(Saigon)

Chola

ASIA

showing current nations and
cities, ancient kingdoms and
relevant indigenous groups

Pallava

Colombo

South China Sea

MALAYSIA

Sarawak

SRI LANKA

Pinang

Batak

Kuala Lumpur

BORNEO

| 0 | 250 | 500 | 750 | 1000 | 1250 | 1500 km |

Kuala Lumpur

SINGAPORE

Minangkabau

Kalimantan

| 0 | 250 | 500 | 750 | 1000 miles |

Indian Ocean

Srivijaya

Sumatra

INDONESIA

Borobudur

Jakarta

Bali

Java

Glossary

bahay na bato	two-storey stone/timber building (Spanish Philippines)
bale	open-sided pavilion (Bali)
bilik	woven bamboo wall (Indonesia)
bundai	low calligrapher's table (Japan)
charpoy	bed of wood and rope (India)
chaw-fa	finials, derived from naga (mythical dragon-snake)
dulang	low table (Philippines)
feng shui	geomancy (China)
fusama	sliding paper screen/internal partition (Japan)
gengkan	entrance lobby (Japan)
irori	sunken hearth (Japan)
jali	lattice screen windows (Mughal India)
jian	unit of space used in Chinese house construction
joglo	ceiling panels raised on pillars (Java)
k'ang	raised platform with heating underneath (China)
kangji	low table for k'ang (China)
kaidan-dansu	stepped cupboards and drawers (Japan)
kotatsu	low rectangular table with heater inside base (Japan)
mandi	wash tank (Indonesia)
noren	banners hung in front of doors (Japan)
oshi-ire	built-in closet (Japan)
pinju pagar	decorative stable-door (Singapore & Malaysia)
qi	life force (China)
ruai	roofed longhouse corridor (Borneo)
Shintoism	Japanese animism and ancestor worship
shoin	study area (Japan)
shoji	sliding external paper wall (Japan)
songket	silk brocade (Malaysia, Indonesia)
ta	day bed (China)
tansu	portable, watertight storage chest (Japan)
tatami	wadded straw and rush mat with bound edges (Japan)
tokonoma	shelved alcove (Japan)
vastu shastra	science of energy (India)
wabi	respect for the intrinsic nature of materials (Japan)
yin & yang	complementary forces of the universe (China)

Origins of Asian Style

Clashing dynasties, imperial patronage, regional colonialization, traders' coffers, spiritual beliefs –
this is the minefield that lies at the heart of that most complex of spectrums, Oriental form.
Aesthetics have always been given high priority in the Orient; so high, indeed, that in the 16th
century Thais were known to go to war over a sculptor or skilled craftsman. Emphasis on the visual
being so determined, the history of Asia can almost be traced through its craftwork: armies may
have failed, but the universal invasion of decorative motifs can be seen in the similarity of designs
and techniques used throughout the region in ceramics, lacquerware, textiles and basketware.

In the beginning there was Buddhism. This was the catalyst for Asia's most visible cultural
migrations and resulted in the diffusion of design techniques and forms over much of the East.
Buddha lived in the 6th century BC, but it took several centuries for the word to radiate southwards
and eastwards from its source in northern India, by which time Buddhist beliefs had merged with a
resurgent Hinduism. Merchants, too, took Indian customs and crafts to every corner of Asia. From
northern India, Buddhism was transported via Nepal and Tibet to China, from where it moved on to
North Vietnam, Korea and Japan; it also travelled south to Sri Lanka and Indonesia, as well as east
through the Khmer kingdom of today's Thailand and Cambodia to present-day southern Vietnam.
Every stage brought permutations and every sojourn led to a variant, but ultimately the common
thread was the Hindu-Buddhist symbolism of the Indian culture.

At Buddhism's core is the cosmic symbol of Mount Meru. This mythological mountain,
surrounded by seven mountain ranges and seven oceans, lies in a walled universe that also contains
four island continents. From this metaphysical design came the mandala, the model for the
symmetrical layout of temples. Also derived from the mandala is the significance given to the centre,
evident in Japanese spatial concepts where the central sunken hearth (*irori*) is traditionally the focal

13

point of the room. Similarly, the bed is positioned in the centre of many contemporary Asian bedrooms. The towering proportions of Mount Meru were reflected in the *chat* (tiered parasol) and funeral pyres of royal Siam, in Balinese temples and in early pagodas of eastern Asia.

Buddhism brought with it an appreciation of space–time relationships, established around five elements (water, fire, wood, metal and earth) and associated with five directions (north, south, east, west and centre), four seasons, and five colours (white, yellow, green, red and blue). In architecture, the bodhi tree under which the Buddha attained enlightenment came to be symbolized in open-sided pavilions, while the river that flowed in front of him gave rise to Asia's enduring emphasis on water.

Building techniques kept pace with the development of Buddhist architectural forms, as with the stupa (shrine), which evolved from India's simple burial mound into the bell shape characteristic of Indo-China. More impressive still was the stupa's vertical growth into multi-storeyed, stone and, later, wooden pagodas, tiered structures that were supported by carved struts with grilled or latticed windows. Nepal, China, Vietnam, Korea and Japan all share this structure. It was again on the back of Buddhism that the domestic architecture of China's Han dynasty (206 BC–AD 220) – with its winged, tiled roofs, profusely decorated ridgepoles and finials, wooden bracketing and columns – was exported from the late 6th century onwards to north Vietnam, Korea and Japan.

DYNAMICS OF THE SILK ROAD

The early centuries of the first millennium AD saw strong injections of Greek and Roman culture, which travelled overland in the wake of Alexander the Great along the Silk Road through the Persian Empire. It was not until the 5th century AD that the Chinese learned the glass-making techniques that Indians had absorbed from the West, and it took another thousand years for the Chinese to adopt the technique of cloisonné enamel. From the West, too, came the silver that resulted in silver goblets for Tang dynasty drinking parties in China, as well as sculptural styles that lent Hellenistic motifs and drapes to Oriental carvings. Similar influences led to the development of a succession of Hellenic, Persian, Indian and Chinese hybrids that continued until the cultural zenith of the Tang dynasty (618–906). In the other direction, the famed caravan routes took silk and, later, porcelain across the deserts of north-west China to Constantinople and thence to Europe. Tributary routes southwards to India strengthened artistic interaction with Central Asia before the Mughals had even arrived.

WATER CULTURE

The sea played a major role in the common design culture of Asia. Sea routes that were established with the first mass migrations after the Ice Age eventually produced the ubiquitous stilt-house and

Above: The gold-leaf and lacquered walls of Kinkakuji, Kyoto's Golden Temple (1400), were faithfully reconstructed after a fire in 1950. The three floors represent the palace style, the samurai house style and that of a Zen temple.

Previous page: The gilded Reclining Buddha at Wat Po, Bangkok, points to the extensive cultural cross-pollination that followed in the steps of Buddhism.

variants like the Thai floating house and even boat-based communities such as the Bajau of the South China Sea. Dwellings among the scattered archipelagos of South-East Asia and along the banks of the great Yangtze or the Mekong rivers and, later, the canals of Bangkok or Banjarmasin, were all shaped by water. And as the winds of the tropical monsoons governed navigation, so the rains themselves determined specific architectural features, notably projecting eaves.

By the 1st century AD, Chinese seafarers were already trading bronze, pottery and coins to countries located to the south, while Indian and Arab boats plied the Indian Ocean laden with ivory, sandalwood and spices. Funan, in what is now Vietnam's Mekong delta, was the first Indianized kingdom outside the subcontinent, and received Hindu-Buddhist input by sea from the 1st to 6th centuries AD before eventually evolving into the great Khmer kingdom based further upriver at Angkor. The most easterly thrust of seaborne Indian culture was the maritime kingdom of Champa, in central Vietnam, whose complex brick tower shrines dedicated to Siva were finally overrun by the Viets in the 15th century.

The first known Oriental design 'export' was the massive Dong Son kettle-drum from northern Vietnam; its intricate motifs and the techniques used in its casting travelled as far as Indonesia during the first millennium BC. Significantly, one of the drum's motifs was a boat-shaped wooden house with an exaggerated, sweeping roofline: this emphasis on the roof form as

Above left: The 17th-century temple of Ulun Danu at Lake Bratan, in Bali, presents tapering pagoda forms with multiple roofs of thatched sugar-palm fibre. *Above right:* Multi-storey Chinese stone pagodas, as seen here in Suzhou, were developed from India's Buddhist stupas from about the 6th century AD. They soon inspired East and South-East Asia's loftiest structures.

The skeletal structure of a Bajau dwelling in the Celebes Sea awaits completion in the form of woven bamboo walls and floor and a thatched roof.

representative of man's closest point to the abode of the gods was to play a defining role in Asian architecture (see pages 25–26).

INDONESIAN FUSION AND DIFFUSION

The first great Buddhist dynasty of South-East Asia was Srivijaya (c.7th–14th centuries). This politically powerful kingdom was highly influential, and disseminated Indianized craft forms and techniques from its base in Sumatra to Java, Borneo, the Malay peninsula, Thailand and Cambodia.

Equally strong in this region were the Hindu dynasties of the Pallavas and Cholas from southern India (together spanning the 4th–12th centuries), which brought architectural styles of carved wood that are still shared by Kerala (southern India), Sri Lanka, the Malay archipelago and parts of Indo-China.

By the 11th century, Java, having fully assimilated these Indian influences, synthesized its own characteristic style under the Hindu-Buddhist Mataram kingdom. This was subsequently reinforced by the highly sophisticated Majapahit dynasty of East Java. As pre-Islamic Javanese culture reached its zenith, brick-making techniques, already used for temples, were perfected and the use of roof tiles became widespread. Despite these advances, the average Javanese house remained a simple bamboo structure and, unlike elsewhere, was ground-built rather than raised on stilts. Majapahit trade links and influences held a tentacular control over most of South-East Asia in the 14th century, but were soon rivalled by the commercial powerhouse of Islamic Melaka in peninsular Malaysia and by the gradual spread of Islam through Sumatra and through Java itself.

Despite injections of Arab influence, Java's deeply rooted animist beliefs and Hindu-Buddhist craft traditions were never eradicated. In fact, in Bali, following the exodus of hardcore Javanese Hindus, the fusion of their culture with existing animism created a particularly rich artistic, ceremonial and architectural heritage. Open-sided pavilions (*bale*), pitched roofs, water palaces, lavish detailing, rich colour and extensive gilding are still the hallmarks of the Balinese approach. The 15th-century Javanese craftsmen, meanwhile, following the Muslim ban on the representation of human figures, instead incorporated calligraphy and vegetal motifs in their superlative woodcarving. Jepara, in particular, became a prolific centre of this craft and soon the houses of the wealthy were entirely composed of prefabricated carved panels. Dutch colonial tastes of the 17th–19th centuries led to hybrid furniture styles, even producing curtain rings carved in the form of the sacred *naga* (mythical dragon-snake). Little has changed since, and decorative detailing is still king, from Sumatra through Java to Bali.

SIAM'S ZENITH

Siam (Thailand) came into its own when the indigenous Mons and Khmers were joined by Thai people from Yunnan in southern China. This gave birth to the brilliant arts and crafts for which the Sukhothai kingdom (*c*.11th–13th centuries) was famous and to Thai styles of art and architecture seen in palaces and houses of ornate woodwork. Not least, Sukhothai saw the genesis of a ceramics industry developed by Chinese potters, although the prehistoric pottery of Ban Chiang, in north-eastern Thailand, is a notable predecessor.

Under the subsequent 400-year reign of the Ayutthaya kingdom, designs and materials evolved from Indian and Khmer sources to reach a zenith of sumptuous gold leaf, tile mosaics, elaborately carved gables, and lacquered murals and doors – the synthesis of an enduring Thai style. In some cases, brick replaced wood, though stilt-houses of wood and bamboo or raft-built, floating houses remained the common lot. As elsewhere, it was only the wealthy echelons of society that adopted elaborately carved furniture in forms adapted from foreign cultures. In general, the Thai contribution to South-East Asian civilization is one of lightness and intricacy, far removed from the heavier approach of the Chinese, the structure of the Japanese or the monumentalism of the Indians.

This corner of a *bale* (pavilion) at the Puri Anyar Krambitan, a 17th-century Balinese palace, exemplifies the local passion for brilliant red and heavily gilded woodcarving.

MALAY PERANAKAN CULTURE

When Chinese junks renewed their domination of the South China Seas in the 11th–15th centuries, China again spread its cultural wings. Ships laden with porcelain, silk, lacquer, silver and gold reached the coasts of Africa, while in 1403 the Ming emperor's trade ambassador, the eunuch Admiral Zheng He, cemented Chinese–Malay relations in Melaka. This sowed the seeds of the prosperous Peranakan culture that thrives today in Melaka, Pinang and Singapore. Under 19th-century British colonial rule the style's hybrid nature was strengthened by a further influx of Chinese migrants as well as by extensive grafting of European architectural features. As a result, Peranakan houses combine traditional Chinese layout, Malay features and neo-Palladian pediments, columns and stuccowork.

VIET STYLES

A similar hybrid time capsule exists at the former port of Faifo (now Hoi An), in central Vietnam, where Japanese and Chinese traders settled in the 16th–17th centuries, producing a wealth of complementary architectural and craft forms. This rare enclave of traders' houses demonstrates the unchanged traditions of prosperous southern Chinese interiors alongside added features such as Japanese crabshell ceilings and Vietnamese furniture. The houses are all built on the shophouse

Above left: The gilded and painted carving of this 17th–18th-century cabinet shows the finesse of Thai workmanship during the reign of the Ayutthaya kingdom. *Above centre:* The Malay-Chinese Peranakan communities excelled at producing blackwood furniture inlaid with mother-of-pearl in Qing dynasty style. Blackwood is in fact a very dark rosewood – the *Dalbergia latifolia*. *Above right:* Turquoise and gold mosaic glitters on the façade of a Thai temple.

Restored late-19th-century shophouses in Singapore's Chinatown demonstrate an amalgam of such European architectural features as fanlights and columns with elements essential to the tropics, including plantation shutters.

model of a deep, narrow building with glazed-tile roof, inner courtyard, ornamental brackets and gables, pivotal doors, carved shutters and wood panelling.

Vietnamese style is particularly difficult to isolate. North Vietnam (Annam) was submerged under Chinese domination until the 10th century, while the south was home to the Khmers, whose graceful finials still dance along temple roofs. Between them lay the Chams and their Indianized culture. However, like Xi'an and Beijing, the successive imperial capitals of Hue and Hanoi nurtured thriving crafts industries (notably lacquer, ceramics and woodcarving) that supplied not only palaces and imperial tombs but also the countless Buddhist temples scattered throughout the countryside.

FILIPINO FULL CIRCLE

Although Filipino links with China were always strong (commerce began as long ago as the 2nd century and tributes were later paid to the Ming emperors by tribal leaders), society was essentially Malay, as is reflected in the Filipinos' stilt-houses, woodcarving, textiles and early pottery. Things changed in the 14th–16th centuries, when the Ming dynasty ban on Chinese sea-trade for political and economic reasons left a vast products vacuum. On the one side, this was filled by Thai

and Viet potters, who had ably learnt ceramics techniques from the Chinese, and on the other by Spanish middlemen who were soon steering galleons loaded with silver bullion from the New World to their new colonial capital of Manila. Increased numbers of Chinese emigrants to the Philippines churned out crafts and furniture for Spanish settlers, and soon Chinese-made silks, carved ivory statues, porcelain and inlaid furniture found their way to the Americas. Thus the East–West dynamic was brought full circle, even producing unexpected cultural spin-offs in certain Mexican designs.

For much of Asia, the process of cultural development changed when the first Portuguese traders entered the arena in the 16th century. The Portuguese were closely followed by the Spanish, then the Dutch and English East India Companies, and finally the French. From then on, the destiny of Oriental design and, to a lesser extent, architecture, was heavily influenced by Western needs and tastes.

KOREA

Although Korea played a major role as cultural intermediary between China and Japan in the early centuries AD, by the mid-7th century its importance had faded. Like the rest of the Far East, Korea lived in the shadow of Chinese art and culture until the arrival of the Mongols in the 10th century,

The interior of the 17th-century Thien Mu monastery in Hue, Vietnam, shows indelible Chinese influences in its moon-windows, complex rafter system and carved ideograms.

when it assumed a pivotal maritime role between the so-called 'barbarian' states of the north and more 'civilized' central China. Koryo dynasty (918–1392) craftsmen excelled in Tang arts, such as lacquer inlaid with mother-of-pearl, and in ceramics, notably celadon, to the extent that examples were presented to the Ming emperor. Korean houses, too, followed the north Chinese model, with tiled, projecting eaves and backs to the bitter north winds. Raised wooden floors concealed underfloor heating similar to the Chinese *k'ang* system (see Glossary, page 11), while windows, inner doors and floors were covered in waxed paper. Like the Japanese, Koreans limited furniture to decorative screens, mats, floor cushions and chests. What is outstandingly different is their fearless use of brilliant colour, both in textiles and architectural features.

JAPANESE RIGOUR

Japan presents a different scenario altogether. Despite pervasive waves of Chinese influence over the centuries, the Japanese sensibility remained distinct. Shintoism, the native animism, imbued the nation with an unrivalled love and respect for nature in its tiniest form (a petal, a grain of sand). From this came a subtle sense of formal beauty, encapsulating balance, purity of line, quality of material and harmony of colour and pattern. Nature is, after all, the original master of form, and Japanese *wabi* (respect for the intrinsic nature of materials) reflects this.

Japan opened its doors to Chinese art and architecture when Mahayana Buddhism (shared by China, Tibet, Korea and northern Vietnam) entered the country via Korea in the 6th century. For three centuries Chinese culture dominated the aristocratic way of life until the demise of the Tang dynasty brought about a resurgence of the native spirit. Structures became more elegant and refined, a reflection of the Japanese affinity with linear art and a far cry from the early houses, which were raised on piles and so ill-adapted to the climate. The art of decoration excelled in delicate interpretations of nature with flat perspectives, while architecture aimed for integration into the landscape, using trees and water as visual extensions to the interior. Stone terraces gave way to verandas for moon-gazing or stream-watching, buildings were connected by covered walkways, and craftsmen created sumptuous interiors of lacquered walls ornamented with gold leaf.

This was not to last, for when relations reopened with China in the 12th century and Ch'an (Zen) Buddhism (developed by a sect of contemplative Chinese monks) was discovered, an entirely new approach took hold. Together with Zen beliefs came the official style of Song dynasty architecture and furnishings. The importance of Zen in the development of Japanese design cannot be understated: its accent on simplicity corresponded perfectly to deeply embedded Shintoism. As Zen spread among the middle class, a new style of home emerged: the *shom-zukuri*. This introduced the *tokonoma* (shelved alcove), a low table, *fusama* (sliding paper screens that were often painted with landscapes), wooden panels, coffered ceilings and the *gengkan* (entrance lobby).

Internal partitions in Asian houses were originally created by placing screens across particular areas as and when required. This six-panelled Japanese example from the late 17th century uses coloured inks and gold-leaf on paper to depict an Edo kabuki theatre – subject-matter that illustrates the breakaway from purely Buddhist imagery.

Although Japanese decorative arts evolved greatly over the next 800 or so years, the essential components of a traditional interior had been established. Once the *tatami* (wadded mat) came into use in the 15th century, the picture was complete. Little was to change during Japan's subsequent self-imposed isolation from foreign influences (c.1637–1853), but with the Restoration of 1868 the floodgates opened. Japanese styles and crafts inundated the West and, in return, brick, iron and stone came to characterize public buildings in Japan. Today, while the purity of traditional Japanese design remains highly influential among minimalist architects of the West, Japanese architects themselves are among the most innovative in the world.

TODAY'S ETHNIC ARCHITECTURE

Climate inevitably affects architectural styles. Think Orient and you naturally think tropics and breezy verandas. However, experience northern China in winter and you will understand why over 40 million people here choose to dig their houses underground. Others adapt to the climate by building in stone, mud or brick and limiting windows to the warmer, south façade. In contrast, the warmer climes of South-East Asia are dominated by wood, crafted into an almost infinite spectrum of styles.

Projecting over pools of still water, the Shintoist shrine of Itsukushima, on the island of Miyajima, is typical of the Shinden style of architecture of the Heian period (782–1185). Rebuilt in 1571, it exemplifies Japanese subtlety and sense of proportion, as well as the significance placed on the roof.

Roof forms

'Often a building is only a roof, columns and floors – the roof dominant, shielding, giving the contentment of shelter. Ubiquitous, pervasively present, the scale or pattern shaped by the building beneath. The roof, its shape, texture and proportion, is the strongest visual factor.' Thus wrote the influential Sri Lankan architect, Geoffrey Bawa, in 1986. It was many centuries earlier, however, that southern China had provided the stylistic urban model for many of the East's ground-built constructions, in which walls are not load-bearing. As a result, incredibly complex roof structures sometimes form an overlapping series, while stylized gables sweep into the air, creating 'swallow's-tail' profiles. Ridgepoles are crowded with symbolic ceramic figures, all of which express the owner's status while conveniently deterring malevolent spirits. More extreme still are the steep roofs of Thailand and Myanmar, where apexes bristle with *chaw-fa* finials, whose form is derived from the *naga* (dragon-snake) of Hindu-Buddhist mythology. It is significant that the Japanese word for roof, *yane*, also means house-root or house-origin.

Sweeping roof forms – along with overhanging eaves, raised floors and verandas – are equally prized by Asia's indigenous builders. Often compared to upturned boats, their houses reach an extravagant extreme among the Minangkabau people of Malaysia and Sumatra, their neighbours

Above left: Extravagantly overlapping roofs extended by sinuous *chaw-fa* finials are synonymous with Thai palace and temple styles, as here at Wat Benjamaborpit, Bangkok. *Above right:* The slightly bulbous form of the gilded stupas of Myanmar is derived from India's original Buddhist shrines, which were simple hemispherical mounds, and from Ceylon's bell-shaped chedi.

Raised plankwalks connect stilt-houses in a timeless water-village of Sabah, Malaysian Borneo. Access is by boat or directly from the land.

the Batak, and the Toraja of Sulawesi. These three minority groups have developed arguably the most decorative and complex forms in Asia. Their soaring roofs are not just for visual impact; they also play an essential role in ventilation as the open-ended gables allow for air flow. In a similar vein, Balinese craftsmen excel at weaving palm-leaf roofs so tightly that water cannot penetrate – but air can.

Lurking beneath the outer edge of these roofs is the veranda, the quintessential Asian structure. Blurring definitions of function, it offers shade from the strong tropical sun, shelter from rain and an intermediary indoor–outdoor living and working space. Not surprisingly, the word 'veranda' itself derives from the Hindi *varanda*, in turn taken from the same Portuguese word, meaning balcony – a further example of the entwinement of East–West cultures over the centuries. And by its very nature the veranda is the perfect expression of an Oriental synthesis of opposites, of indoor and out, of yin and yang.

Stilt-houses of the tropics

Rural regions from the Philippines through Indo-China to south China, southern Japan, the Malay archipelago and Thailand are peppered with thatched, wooden houses raised on piles. Stilt-houses have been around Asia for a long time, as proved by their depiction on Chinese bronze drums of the early centuries AD and a bas-relief at Java's 9th-century temple of Borobudur. Far more suited than ground-built houses to excessive heat, rain and floods, and providing protection against wild animals or aggressive neighbours, stilt-houses also successfully withstand earthquakes. Standing in lagoons and on riverbanks, or clustered in coastal water-villages, they are accessed via plankwalks or by ladder directly from boats. An extreme form can be seen in the riverside longhouses of Borneo, which accommodate up to thirty Dayak families under one roof in a unique system of communal living. In Thailand, the central plains and the Lanna region of the north had their own model of 'cluster' house, entirely raised on piles. Meanwhile, Malay kampungs are geared to nuclear family units – although they are still high above the ground.

Prefabrication and transformation

South-East Asia's rural houses have always been transportable, a feature made necessary by floods, soil erosion, war or the search for better farming land. Prefabricated walls of split bamboo or wood can be dismounted from their frame and rapidly re-erected elsewhere. Linguistic proof of this is that *prung*, the Thai word for house building, also means to assemble. Equally, a house can be modified according to need. Japan's sliding screens and walls epitomize versatile interiors, while chickblinds (of reed or split bamboo) or free-standing, movable screens shield inhabitants from sunlight, rain and draughts. The ultimate transportable Asian housing structure is, of course, the tent, still widely used in Central Asia and northwest China by nomadic peoples, who are able to erect a fully furnished yurt in under an hour.

Where wealth and space are often at a premium, transformation and versatility are integral to the way people live. So the emphasis in these situations is on storage systems such as chests or jars, either folding furniture or no furniture and, above all, the absence of compartmentalized space. This can be living at its simplest level, when a sleeping mat stored in a corner is unrolled in an area already used for eating and socializing. In Japan, the emphasis on the visual absence of personal possessions stems from Buddhist tenets of transformation and Zen purity. A more prosaic version of transformation is demonstrated in an urban context by Singaporeans, who use their apartment-block balconies not for relaxing on, but for hanging out washing. For, despite their high-tech society, Singaporeans cling to an age-old preference for air-dried clothes suspended on bamboo poles.

Chinese wooden trunks with ornate brass lock plates remain essential home accessories for storage and transportation.

27

HOUSE RITUALS

Buddhism is far from being the only spiritual belief in the East. Hinduism, Confucianism, Taoism, Islam and various forms of animism have all held sway in different regions – sometimes they have even merged – giving rise to numerous rituals and specific features of domestic interiors. Without a basic understanding of them, it is impossible to fathom some of the key factors in traditional Asian houses.

Feng shui

The oldest esoteric system is feng shui (literally meaning wind and water), widely practised in Singapore, Malaysia, Taiwan, Hong Kong and mainland China after more than four thousand years. The system of creating optimum building conditions, orientation and layout originated in the notion of yin and yang, the complementary forces that govern the universe and produce qi, the cosmic energy or life force. This doctrine stemmed from the second millennium BC *I-Ching* (the *Book of Changes*), and was later integrated into Taoism, whose aim is for each individual to find balance and seek oneness with the Tao – the 'path' or 'original principle'.

A shrine dedicated to Zaojun, the kitchen god, reigns over the cooking area of a house in Hoi An, Vietnam. Incense is lit daily.

Armed with topographical diagrams and the astrological charts of prospective residents, the feng shui geomancer makes complex on-site calculations to determine even minor aspects of the house. Many of the tenets appear to be common sense, such as erecting south-facing houses with their back against the mountain, avoiding building on marshes, choosing the proximity of auspicious water (preferably flowing) and constructing projecting eaves to block high sun rays in summer and to allow low winter rays to penetrate. Less straightforward conditions give rise to bamboo or trees planted behind houses as windbreaks, while the geomancer's detection of dragon lines (underground energy lines), less evident to the uninitiated, is paramount.

In line with this, the Chinese use endless ploys to encourage good fortune and fend off malevolent spirits. In architectural terms, the spirit wall is the most visible, as this stands parallel to the main entrance in order to deflect negative elements, which are considered incapable of travelling round corners. Similarly, external walkways should not be straight but should zigzag. A small mirror hung over the front door serves the same deflective purpose. Inside, Taoist deities such as Zaojun, the kitchen god, are honoured with individual altars, although pride of place goes to the family, or ancestral, altar in the entrance hall. This particular custom stems from Confucianism, a body of moral teachings that originated in 6th–5th-century BC China. Its strong emphasis on filial loyalty, education and respect for government and for ancestors has left an indelible mark on the Chinese psyche, although this often merges confusingly with Taoism and Mahayana Buddhism. Luckily for the evolution of interior design, Confucius did say, 'In the dwelling of a true gentleman, what unrefinement can there be?'

An essential element in traditional Chinese house-construction is the building module of *jian*, meaning the space between two columns, as well as a volumetric space defined by columns, floor and beams. This module is always used in auspicious, odd numbers, one *jian* being the most basic and three or five the most common – a belief also followed in Thailand.

Balinese and Thai rituals

Possibly the most idiosyncratic of Asian orientation systems is that of the Balinese. Their spiritual focus is the volcano, Mount Agung, considered home to numerous gods who, together with the Hindu trinity of Brahma, Vishnu and Siva, are worshipped and placated on a daily basis. Villages and walled family compounds are all built on an axis that relates to the holy mountain (*kaja*) and to the sea (*kelod*), home to a host of local demons and therefore inauspicious. Orientation towards the rising sun in the east (*kangin*) is considered preferable to orientation towards the setting sun in the west (*kauh*) and, as in Buddhism's cosmic plan of Mount Meru, the centre (*puseh*) holds equal

Chinese ancestor portraits, often combining several generations, proliferated during the Ming dynasty (1368–1644). Each region produced a different painterly style although they all stemmed from Confucianism's emphasis on ancestral respect.

importance. As a result, houses are divided into three sections: the family temple; the living quarters; and the more prosaic sections of kitchen, rubbish and animal pen at the *kelod* end. Taking this even further, the Balinese respect auspicious places to eat and to have sexual intercourse and the direction in which to lie down to sleep.

In terms of complexity Thai rituals follow closely, and are strongly reminiscent of, Chinese practices. Before a house is built, astrologers are consulted and, as with the Balinese, there are strict rules concerning alignment. Here, too, the east of the rising sun is sacred, while the west represents death and impurity. Meanwhile, the auspicious north is associated with the elephant, the creature of royalty. On this basis, bedrooms should never be in the west, which is the domain of cooking and washing. Bedrooms occupy the highest level of a house and all doors and windows must open inwards. Odd numbers win over even ones, determining the number of rungs in a ladder or steps in a staircase, as well as the number of spaces between posts. When someone moves into a house, complex rituals ensure the cleansing of spirits and future good fortune, a practice shared by almost every other South-East Asian society.

India's vastu shastra

Closely linked to feng shui, and an influential precursor of the Balinese and Thai systems, is the ancient Indian *vastu shastra*, the 'science of energy'. This originated three thousand years ago in the Stapatya Vedas in order to provide principles for construction in harmony with the five elements of sky, earth, water, fire and wind. By extension, the principles can be applied to commercial buildings and even to entire cities. As every dwelling is enclosed, energy is generated by the inhabitants and their astrological birth-charts. The gods, of course, enter the equation. Eight of them are identified as corresponding to the cardinal directions and their mid-points: east, the number one god, brings wealth and all pleasures; south-east, fire, governs the growth of personality; south, death, eradicates evil; south-west dispenses with fear of enemies; west, rain, brings prosperity and pleasure through showers; north-west, wind, brings health and longevity; and north brings wealth.

The numerous permutations of the above systems go well beyond mere orientation and are far too complex to enter into here. What is clear, however, is that even today Asia is riddled with beliefs and rituals regarding house-construction and internal layout. A Malay newspaper will, for example, contain an agony page devoted, not to problems of the heart, but to problems arising from bad feng shui. Less convincingly, a recent Indian *vastu shastra* manual (1996) acknowledges technological progress in the author's discourse on the telephone. As it is connected to power, the telephone should be located in the fire corner and, above all, far from any water source, water being the antithesis of fire. The author predicts that any water, even a cup of tea, coming close to the phone will result in wrong numbers or no connection – perhaps proof that some Oriental systems need serious updating!

FURNITURE EVOLUTION

It was Chinese ingenuity in developing greater domestic comfort that spearheaded the Asian transition from mat-level living. The oldest known furniture (wooden and bamboo beds, low tables, chests, storage boxes, screens), excavated from Chu kingdom tombs of the 3rd–4th centuries BC, is surprisingly sophisticated. Decorated with painted or carved lacquer, whose broad palette of colours included gold and silver, all the pieces were low-level to accommodate the tradition of kneeling. Hinge mechanisms meant they could be folded away or could have doors that closed. Some pieces incorporated decorative bronze corners, openwork carving or inlaid jade. New forms appeared in the 5th–6th centuries AD, when the Chinese relaxed their formal manner of kneeling and finally sat up straight on stools, chairs or benches, often around long tables. By the time of the Song dynasty

Classical Ming chairs represented the apogee of Chinese furniture and the culmination of over 1,500 years of development. Always made in pairs, these horseshoe chairs are constructed from the much sought-after *huanghuali* (a rosewood). Chairs belonging to important people were draped with furs and/or decorative textiles.

31

(960–1279) the prototypes of today's high furniture had spread to every level of society, leaving the path open for the acme of Chinese design under the Ming (1368–1644).

The general prosperity of the Ming period and the relaxation of imperial demands on artisans freed up carpenters and cabinet makers to accommodate the demands of an expanding middle class. When trade was resumed with South-East Asia in the late 16th century, giving Cantonese artisans access to fine tropical hardwoods, a greater refinement appeared in design, and bamboo was relegated to the lower echelons. This period, the high point of classical Ming furniture, produced the archetypal horseshoe armchair, the yokeback side-chair, folding chairs inlaid with agate, tables with marble tops, canopied beds, couches, footstools, cabinets, display cases and bookcases. Honey-coloured *huanghuali* was the tropical wood of choice, closely followed by *jichimu*, the coarser *tieli*, and *jumu*, a variety of Asian elm. Blackwood (actually a dark rosewood) became widely used under the Qing dynasty (1644–1911).

Under the second Qing emperor, Kangxi, workshops were set up in the Forbidden City of Beijing for a multitude of crafts, from enamels to glass, porcelain, weaving, ivory and gemstones. Foreign Jesuits were employed, particularly in the glass and enamel workshops, bringing Western input to designs and techniques. Qing dynasty furniture became increasingly ornate, with elaborate inlays and carving sometimes resulting in heavy, cumbersome designs that were a far cry from Ming elegance.

No other country in Asia placed such a continuous emphasis on furniture. India's elaborate designs developed only under Turkish and Mughal (Central Asian) rule from the 13th century onwards, and Thailand's, at Ayutthaya, came under the influence of foreign travellers and traders in the 15th–16th centuries. In turn, Japan's minimal pieces were offshoots of early Korean and Chinese models. Of the indigenous cultures, it was the Filipinos who revelled in a sole item of furniture, the multi-purpose *dulang*. This low, rectangular table made of a single plank of wood, or bamboo strips bound by rattan, was used for food preparation, eating or game-playing, and would be moved around the room accordingly. Its inspiration was undoubtedly the Chinese *kangji*, a low table designed for the multi-functional *k'ang* platform. In general, however, furniture remained restricted to the upper echelons of society and was essentially derivative of Chinese styles until the influence of the West began to be felt from the 16th century onwards. Portuguese, Spanish, Dutch and English colonists became adept at importing European prototypes to be copied by Asian craftsmen, inspiring new local forms as well as hybrids such as the planter's chair.

In the West, meanwhile, the importing of exotic hardwoods, notably ebony and mahogany, together with inlay materials of ivory, tortoiseshell and mother-of-pearl, all transformed the face of

Opposite: Colours of jade and vermilion: a contrast of complementaries and a superlative example of a Thai celadon vase at the Suan Pakkad palace in Bangkok.

Above: Lacquering wood to a high gloss was an Oriental technique adopted by art deco designers in Paris of the 1920s and 1930s. These modernist occasional tables designed by Eileen Gray in 1927 are now produced by Aram Designs.

Opposite: Honest materials (chengal timber, siltstone, raw silk and bamboo) and balanced proportions make this Singaporean living room designed by SCDA a perfect example of contemporary East–West fusion. Lightness and serenity are the keynotes.

European furniture, while dining tables groaned under Chinese blue-and-white exportware. Equally influential were techniques such as Indian caning for chairs, far better adapted to humidity than upholstery, and lacquering, known as japanning. Lacquerwork had become popular in 17th-century France and England in the form of magnificent chests and cabinets, but it was during the following century that Oriental influences exploded into chinoiserie, a Western pastiche that sometimes gave a completely warped view of the original aesthetic. Whimsical, asymmetrical 'Oriental' motifs crowded European interiors, while Chinese silks proliferated in curtains, bed-hangings and upholstery. Painted wallpapers, although not a Chinese tradition, were nevertheless genuinely 'made in China'. More subtle influences came in the form of openwork carving of mid-18th-century Chippendale chairs and cabinet doors.

The following century saw a further revival of Eastern passions in the form of bamboo, cane and rattan furniture. Even beechwood was carved and painted to imitate bamboo. Lacquered French art deco furniture of the 1920s and 1930s, exemplified by Eileen Gray's streamlined designs, again brought Oriental techniques to the forefront of Western attention. At the beginning of the 21st century, as Western interiors emphasize more sensual and honest materials, Asia's vast spectrum of sources and forms continues to inspire. The wheel of East–West fusion will no doubt spin indefinitely.

Spatial
Divisions

However open to the elements and versatile the Asian home may be, it still demands a basic structure. The countless variants found across this vast region are tributaries of climate, culture and available resources, but certain features, materials and treatments occur again and again: woven split-bamboo walls; slatted, carved, latticed, fretted and/or panelled wood; pillars; revealed rafters and beams; lightwells; shutters; blinds; and sliding, swing or pivoting doors. Fused with these traditional features are those brought by erstwhile colonizers: louvred shutters; fanlights; *jali*; screen windows (an Islamic import into Mughal India); stucco wall decoration; the half-timbered British style of Singapore's 'black-and-white' houses and Malaysia's colonial bungalows; and the two-storey *bahay na bato* of stone and timber that was developed in the Spanish Philippines.

Whether made of rammed earth, mud, bamboo, timber, brick or stone, the walls of an Asian house are an elusive element that comes and goes with the choreography of circulation and climate. In relation to exterior space, it is often a case of 'now you see it, now you don't' as partitions slide invisibly away or blinds are rolled out of sight. It is not unusual to see a Javanese farmer trotting down the road beneath a voluminous *bilik* (woven bamboo wall) that is destined to be mounted on the basic frame of his house. *Bilik* can be as complex in their design as textiles, their elaborate patterns created with different coloured bamboo or paint. An outstanding example of the regional cross-currents are the intricately carved and painted gables of Sumatra's Minangkabau people, which are thought to have been inspired by imported Chinese brocades. Closer to their own roots, the Toraja's decorative wall-panels are incised and painted with stars, spirals and buffalo heads.

Throughout South-East Asia, much pride is taken in the fact that not a single nail was used in traditional constructions; instead, dowels and pegs, together with rattan binding, held wall and beam structures together. This system allowed constructions to be dismantled, replaced or

re-erected without any damage. Today, a renewed enthusiasm for traditional elements means that wall panels and pillars have been salvaged from demolished constructions and are being successfully integrated into new houses.

Urban structures differ from rural ones, and Japanese form from Indo-Chinese, but the underlying predilection for local resources and ventilation systems was a common one until the advent of ceiling fans and the intervention of 20th-century technology. Attempts at air-conditioning were made as early as the 8th century, when the cold-water circulation of the palace of Xi'an was so successful that ministers caught cold while in audience with the Emperor Hsuan Tsung. He, of course, was sufficiently well clad. Less extreme ventilation systems, such as open-ended gables or water pools, are now being revived in contemporary houses. For, despite the widespread bulldozing of the majority of traditional houses in the cities of Beijing, Bangkok, Singapore and Jakarta, the tide has turned. Respect for the environmental intelligence of ancient techniques is producing sophisticated modern versions.

WALLS AND WINDOWS

In the colder parts of the Far East, windows were traditionally scarce and generally were placed only on the warmer, southern façade. Wooden lattices covered with oil-paper were the norm in northern

Three types of partition reveal the versatile applications of Bali's indigenous materials. *Above left:* Framed woven bamboo panels at the Chedi Hotel give a contemporary look to an age-old tradition. *Above centre:* Balinese sugar-palm thatch is transformed into tiles by Linda Garland to create a textural outdoor partition. *Above right:* A classic chickblind of split bamboo reinforced with binding.

Opposite: A traditional Chinese screen, its upper sections formed of openwork carving, creates a mobile partition that emphasizes light and a sense of space.

Previous page: A generous entrance porch to a house in Singapore contrasts neo-modernist planes and latticed screens with the evocative and fugitive qualities of water and filtered sunlight.

China and Korea, comparable to, though not the same as, the Japanese *shoji*, which generates that inimitable translucence. Chinese clay window grilles became an art form in themselves, varying in complexity according to prosperity and the desired symbolism. This feature reappears in contemporary houses as ventilation grilles, although the extraordinary whimsy both of pattern and window shape has been lost. For Chinese windows varied from fan-shaped to vase-shaped, from octagonal to circular – the latter an echo of South-East Chinese moon-gates, which migrated with the Chinese diaspora.

The constant temperatures of the tropics means that window-openings can be unglazed to allow breezes and cross-ventilation. This advantage has been widely exploited by the Kerala-based architect, Laurie Baker, in his environmentally sensitive, low-cost, brick houses. Their windows are actually a geometric pattern of apertures that allow air-circulation yet deter intruders. At the very most, Baker inserts recycled coloured glass in overt homage to Mughal traditions. This same technique of patterned openings is found in some traditional Balinese walls.

In Thailand, windows were traditionally closed and bolted by solid wooden shutters; in the upper echelons of society these were densely decorated with painted and gilded carving. As a security device, carved wooden bars often filled the opening, a system that is still common throughout South-East Asia. More elaborate was the Javanese version of openwork carving, where

Circular forms are an omnipresent Asian characteristic echoing the Chinese moon-gate, which symbolized perfection and the saying 'Be round without but be square within'. *Above left:* A classic moon-window offers a view to a neighbouring shopfront in a 'five-footway' in Melaka, Malaysia. *Above centre:* Chinese plates are inserted into a rendered wall at Bali's Puri Merta, reviving an old Majapahit tradition. *Above right:* In Bangkok, a circular mirror reflects Bill Bensley's terrace birdcage collection.

Opposite: An interior opening at Lajeunesse Asian Art gallery, Singapore, frames a row of Burmese *hsun-ok* (offering vessels), with *chaw-fa* finials in the foreground.

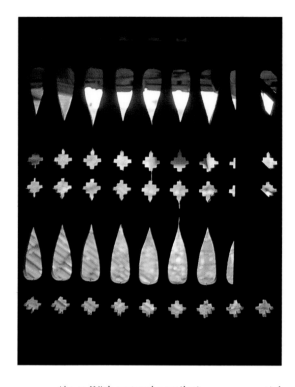
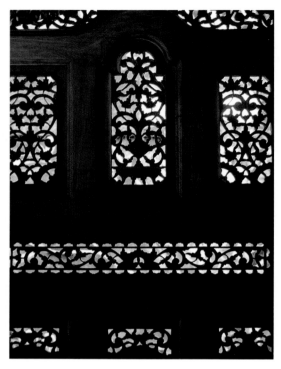

Above: With natural ventilation an esssential component to the structure, Asian styles of working wooden walls vary from fretwork (*left*) and curved slats (*right*), both at the 16th–18th-century palace of Padmanabhapuram in southern India, to intricate filigree carving in Mughal style (*centre*), a Javanese talent exemplified in this reconstructed 19th-century Kudus pavilion at the Begawan Giri, Bali.

Opposite: Soaring ceilings, as seen here in the Tugu Hotel's lobby, have become the hallmark of contemporary Balinese style. Revealed between the rafters, the underside of the thatched roof allows air to penetrate, while lateral sunlight is filtered through white gauze curtains.

the Islamic influence created a filigree silhouette that echoed the profuse carvings of brackets, beams, columns and wall panels. Although less intricate, the lattice and/or carved bars of southern Indian palaces also produced an extraordinary visual array.

Also varying in complexity according to social status, the Thai style of panelled wood walls is thought to date back 300 years. One theory for its popularity is that it facilitated an assembly-line process of prefabrication while also being an economical way of using leftover wood.

More colourful was the treatment given to outdoor walls by the Balinese: in the tradition of the Majapahit dynasty (14th–15th centuries), ceramics were inserted into the brickwork. A consequence of this practice was that Bali unexpectedly became a destination for Vietnamese exportware and Ming porcelain. The technique has been revived in Made Wijaya's design of the Puri Merta hotel in Bali, creating contrasting texture and pattern in rendered brick gateways that lead to garden courtyards.

The walls of rural houses in Japan, if they were not made of richly lacquered panels, paper or wood, were constructed by applying layers of clay to both sides of a bamboo framework; for a superior, luminous interior finish, sand would be mixed with ground seaweed and crushed pearl. *Fusama* (internal partitions) were often the only visible expression of wealth as their thick paper covering could receive printed patterns, murals or calligraphy.

1

2

Right: Walls that take on texture yet allow ventilation and light. *(1)* Broad strips of merbau wood woven like bamboo. *(2)* Traditional Chinese openwork. *(3)* Pivoting louvred screens edged with steel to prevent warping and set a metre in front of a glazed wall in Singapore. *(4)* Ripple-shaped slits in a screen partition at Bali's Chedi Hotel.

Opposite: The entrance pavilion at Nagara's multi-pavilion home in Bangkok combines reproductions of traditional Chinese carved doors with glazed walls that can be shaded by fine slatted blinds. The latter allow a choice between interior shadow or views onto the luxuriant water garden.

3

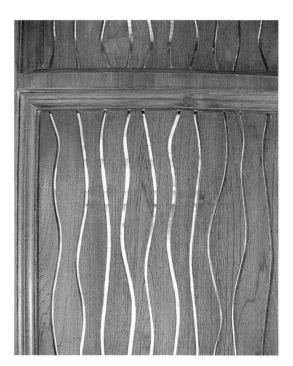

4

Inspired by the tradition of woven split bamboo, more sophisticated walls are today woven from broad strips of thin merbau. This creates a textured yet even appearance and, again, functions well for ventilation purposes. Linda Garland, the 'bamboo queen' of Bali, has also developed charcoal-coloured tiles of sugar-palm thatch for partition walls (see page 39). Other contemporary developments are found at Bali's Chedi Hotel, which maximizes the use of fixed screens containing ripple-shaped slits. Here, too, woven bamboo set in geometrical frames gives a contemporary look and a more solid structure to an age-old tradition.

Glazing took a long time to replace traditional window coverings, but now, throughout contemporary Asia, it is used widely and generously. Distinctions between walls, doors and windows become blurred as full-length, glazed panels either slide, pivot or fold in concertina fashion to bring the outside in. When privacy or a shield from strong sunlight is required, other materials come into play. This is where the Japanese *shoji* (a sliding paper wall) comes into its own as it diffuses light and casts evocative shadows from outside while being lightweight enough to slide easily or to be removed entirely. If the appropriate paper (traditionally made from the mulberry tree or the thyme plant) is neither available nor practical, a post-industrial alternative is to use panels of opaque acrylic, an economical equivalent to acid-etched glass.

Simple lattice panels are another option, echoing the Japanese sliding *shoji* when they are made with flat horizontals and the *jali* screens of Mughal India when diagonals are used. Diamonds of sunlight cast on the floor are a seductive visual spin-off of this system. Lattice also appears as textural interest when laid over an existing wood panel and painted in the same colour – cinnabar red being the obvious Oriental choice. However, the ultimate reinterpretation of an Asian classic is the louvred timber wall, which allows permanently adjustable natural ventilation and light. This has been developed by architects such as Ernesto Bedmar and Chan Soo Khian in Singapore.

BLINDS, SCREENS AND BANNERS

The gamut of Asian window coverings includes what perhaps qualifies as the world's first blind: strings of dried tobacco leaves suspended from the eaves – an old south Chinese pipe-smokers' habit. A few steps up in standard and offering moody variations on light and shade are louvred shutters (sometimes opening in vertical flap fashion), slatted wooden blinds and bamboo chickblinds, the latter having the added atmospheric interest of movement in the breeze. More sumptuous in style and in tune with cooler climes or air-conditioned rooms is the multiplication of curtains with extravagant abandon. Even if the curtains are rarely untied, the repetition of soft cotton folds can punctuate an otherwise monotonous corridor, as seen at Linda Garland's

Above: Privacy is a problem in densely populated Singapore. It is solved in this bedroom by a combination of cotton Roman blinds that impart a translucent light and a movable carved screen that adds a graphic dimension.

Opposite: Masters of the art of muted light and versatile living, the Japanese also excel at harmonious proportions. In this contemporary interior, sliding paper walls bring the exterior in or shade it out, while the ceiling height is calculated according to the number of *tatami* mats.

home in Bali. More extreme still, repeated swathes of shimmering Thai silk, floor-to-ceiling curtains will, with the right nocturnal lighting, give the magical sensation of being inside a Mughal tent.

Before fixed partitions were ever used, freestanding screens were the norm in China, Korea and Japan. A lengthy existence has spawned variations that include sumptuous lacquer, openwork carving, rice-paper and contemporary versions in bamboo or rattan. Other space-dividers, which originated in Japan, are *noren*, suspended cloth banners traditionally hung in front of doors, or bamboo blinds. Either offers instant changes in the volumetric composition of a room. This system has been reinterpreted by the Thai fashion-designer Nagara in his entrance pavilion, where two vertical banners of Buddhist iconography hang inside the main doorway, producing a dramatic though impermanent effect.

DOORS

Oriental doors range from simple affairs of bound or woven bamboo and plain timber to carved, gilded, delicately painted, lacquered, openwork or inlaid versions. The mother-of-pearl inlay seen in parts of Indonesia is undoubtedly an Arab import, while in China openwork carving sometimes fills circular 'moon' openings or may be incorporated into tall, narrow doors that swing open on dowel

Above left: Steep overhangs shielding upper-floor rooms from the overhead sun are supported in Mrs Leonara Tan's Singapore house by slanting, slatted brackets in the pagoda style. *Above right:* The same house employs an adjustable louvred wall – each slat handcrafted – to banish driving rain or hot air from the interior.

Opposite: A rarity in the tropics, linen curtains punctuate what could otherwise be a monotonous corridor of Linda Garland's Balinese house. Further definition comes in the form of traditional raised door-jambs.

1

2

Door features of Asia vary considerably with climate and location. (1) The structure of this simple Korean example is emphasized by overhead calligraphy and by its alignment with a floor-to-ceiling window beyond. (2) Rustic Balinese style produces a woven bamboo door that harmonizes with the walls and thatched roof. (3) In Kyoto, Japan, a tiled overhang shields callers from rain while curved bamboo strips protect the external drain. (4) Typical of Singapore's conservation houses is the *pinju pagar*, a stable door that gives inhabitants privacy yet allows ventilation when the main front door is left open.

3

4

1

2

3

4

(1) Another version of a *pinju pagar* incorporates coloured-glass inserts to the varnished stable door to increase interior light. *(2)* More soberly contemporary, this louvred door in Singapore continues the tropical preoccupation with natural ventilation. *(3)* At Bali's Chedi Hotel, a simple shutter inserted into the beam structure lets in the morning light or keeps out the evening mosquitoes. *(4)* In a juxtaposition of solidity and lightness at the 17th–18th-century Suan Pakkad Palace in Bangkok, a heavy wooden door highlighted by decorative gilding opens onto a corridor of lacquered walls flooded with sunlight.

At this Singapore house, designed by HYLA Architects for Mr and Mrs John Tan, glazed doors fold back in concertina style to let the cooling air and reflections of water flood the living room. A Javanese couch and table, a Chinese bench and Sri Lankan side tables complete the pan-Asian style.

pins. In Borneo, more whimsical designs exist in the Dayak peoples' hardwood doors, often carved with huge lizards and other animist symbols.

In the traditional architecture of South-East Asia, front doors are often double, raised above a threshold or frame and closed with a sturdy wooden bolt. This style exists from Kerala to Indo-China in temples and in homes. In Java, Bali and Thailand, carved panels are also painted and/or gilded. Balinese doors often incorporate small ventilation grilles and are generally surmounted by a high-relief decorative frieze – more often than not depicting the globular-eyed god Bhoma. This form of woodcarving is where Balinese craftsmen excel. Their richly carved and gilded interior door frames

in hotel suites at the Tugu and the Puri Merta, both in Bali, create a regal and exotic note in the graduation from sitting room to bedroom. In contrast, internal doors in neo-modernist Asian houses are often Japanese in inspiration, harmonizing geometric, sliding latticework with minimalist interiors.

Vegetal, floral or geometric patterns characterize the Chinese openwork woodcarving of front and inner doors. In shophouses the vegetal motif is often echoed by a decorative filigree fanlight above the door (a form borrowed from colonial styles) or is contrasted with louvred panels set into the door itself. Typical of the Peranakan style in Singapore and Malaysia is the *pinju pagar* (stable door), which provides privacy and ventilation when the main security door behind is open. The *pinju*

pagar's decorative appeal has raised it to an extremely colourful status symbol in Singapore's Chinatown and Emerald Hill districts.

CEILINGS

With so much emphasis placed on the roof throughout the Orient, ceilings and their supports are inevitably important. From rural Japan to southern India the complex rafter structures remain revealed. In Bali, the dramatic effect of soaring *alang alang* roofs held aloft by solid ironwood pillars is such that they have multiplied among contemporary houses and hotels. Seen from within, these thatched roofs present a regular horizontal pattern of tightly bound grass whose natural tones blend with furnishings of wood, bamboo or rattan. Linda Garland's Balinese bedroom is a prime example, its lofty height emphasized by the cross-beam structure, a towering Asmat carving and a voluminous mosquito net – all on a startling scale. It is also common in South-East Asia to leave the undersides of tiled roofs exposed between wooden rafters, although sometimes these are concealed by timber or rush matting.

In palatial Balinese *bale* (pavilions) gilded demons and gods are carved into the beams, and pillars culminate in stylized lotus capitals and bases. Chinese, Vietnamese and Javanese ceilings all share this taste for carving and colour, however much these works of art become lost in the

Above left: An intriguing revival of a traditional Balinese *cartagosa* (meeting pavilion) is found here at the Tugu Hotel. The canopy defines a sitting area, all of which lies beneath the classic underside of a thatched roof. *Above right:* The *joglo*, a Javanese system of inserted ceiling panels supported by slender columns, is designed to emphasize the importance of the entrance hall. It is used here at Sandrine Soimaud's Balinese house as a feature in the master bedroom.

Opposite: A *mbis*, an Asmat ancestor pole, rises into the heights of Linda Garland's Balinese bedroom, its imposing scale echoed by a billowing mosquito net. This softening feature swings gently on its suspended poles when helped by the breeze of a ventilator.

1

2

Ceiling-building techniques emphasize the significance of the roof in Asian architecture, where brackets and rafters are highly complex works of art imbued with symbolic and spiritual significance. *(1)* A Japanese crabshell ceiling in an 18th-century trader's house in Hoi An, Vietnam. *(2)* The Balinese god Bhoma gazes down from a rafter at the Puri Anyar Krambitan palace in Bali. *(3)* Repetitive use of intricately carved brackets creates a decorative rhythm in this 150-year-old Kudus pavilion from Java, reconstructed at the Begawan Giri. *(4)* Ornately carved struts and beams in the same Kudus pavilion.

3

4

1

2

3

4

(1) Split bamboo matting lining a shingle roof creates a texturally uniform ceiling at Kathy Kamei's house in Bali. *(2)* The Korean love of vivid colour juxtapositions, shared by the Mongols and Central Asians, comes to the fore in this handpainted ceiling of a temple gateway at Suwon, South Korea. *(3)* These 300-year-old Balinese carved rafters contrast with the more banal asbestos ceiling grid at the Puri Anyar Krambitan palace, Bali. *(4)* A wood-panelled ceiling, animated by the whirr of a fan, offers a minimalist edge to a modern Balinese house.

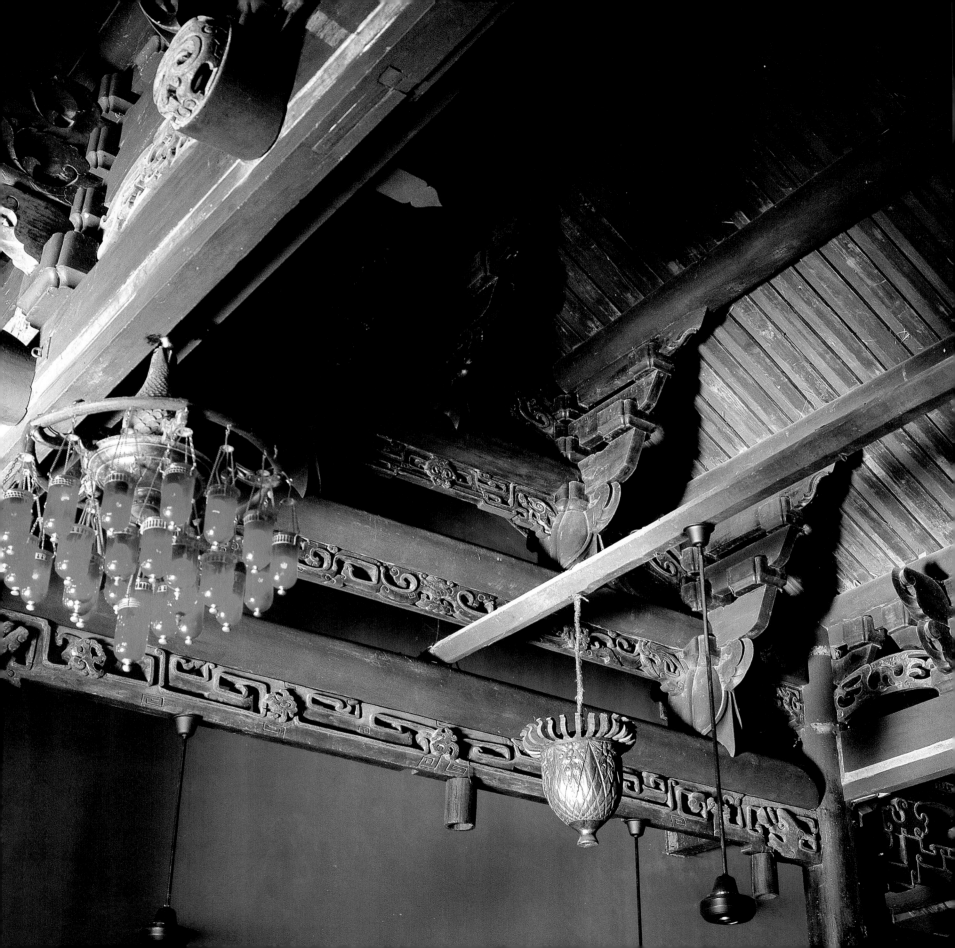

shadowy heights. A traditional Javanese pavilion reconstructed at the Begawan Giri demonstrates the mastery of 19th-century woodcarvers and also the extent to which decorative detail was concentrated in the upper part of the building. Also typical of the Chinese strut-and-beam systems, which held the entire weight of the roof, is the ceiling of the Tugu hotel's reconstructed Chinese temple, dating from 1706. In these structures, walls are mere enclosures without any supporting function. Revealed pillar-and-lintel structures are also common in traditional rural houses of Japan, although coffered ceilings became widespread in the late 15th century. Ever refined, the Japanese based ceiling height on the size of the room seen from a mat-level perspective. Elsewhere in Asia, flat ceilings incorporated panels or were coffered, and some were lacquered or decorated with carved details, as found in the wealthy old houses of Thailand.

A Javanese ceiling innovation was the *joglo*, composed of a pair of carved panels set in a square ceiling frame and raised on four pillars. Designed as a form of structural canopy above entrance halls, this feature has been successfully resurrected by Sandrine Soimaud in her Balinese home (see page 55). Similar in concept is the Tugu's use of a canopied area within a room; in a stylistic nod to the *cartagosa* (Balinese meeting pavilion), a room within a room is created with this double ceiling of rich vermilion and gold fabric below the classic underside of *alang alang* (elephant grass) thatch.

Lofty ceilings reappear in Singapore's converted shophouses, where double height brings drama and skylights illuminate internal pools. This is a variant on the traditional lightwell, the principal source of ventilation that varied in scale from large internal courtyards of Chinese and Vietnamese houses to more modest openings that merely fulfilled the function of air circulation. Sri Lankan and Keralan houses also incorporated a large, open-roofed area with lateral eaves directing the torrential monsoon rain into a pool. Sri Lankan architect Geoffrey Bawa famously resurrected this traditional feature in the 1960s and it reappears in contemporary houses in Singapore.

FLOORS

A sober background to the complexities of ceilings and walls, the Asian floor is the least emphatic element of the shell. Perhaps the only characteristic that could be said to be specifically Asian is differentials in level. Used most commonly in Japan, interior graduations of level are, once again, a subtle method of suggesting and accommodating change.

In traditional stilt-houses, floors made of timber planks or bamboo facilitate sweeping and washing, as crumbs drop below to the animal domain or into water. Further up the economic scale you find gleaming, polished floors of tropical wood from Thailand to Java, Malaysia to Vietnam, Myanmar to the Philippines. However, with environmental concerns high on today's agenda, the beautiful grains

Above: A superbly carved rosewood casement ceiling at the 16th–18th-century Padmanabhapuram palace in southern India incorporates ninety different carved lotuses.

Opposite: Chinese craft techniques spread all over Asia with economic emigrants. This Kang Xi family temple (1706), originally built in Java but now reconstructed at Bali's Tugu Hotel, demonstrates the skilled workmanship that went into ceiling rafters. The bulbous red-glass lamps, a form that originated in India, now exist in varying colours throughout Asia.

Above left: Terracotta 'Bali-tiles' provide textural contrast to a split-bamboo mat and a woven bamboo floor cushion at the Villa Melati, Bali. *Above centre:* The same house offers seamless circulation through numerous openings and raised levels. The flooring is of Bali-tiles and merbau wood. *Above right:* Tongue-and-groove flooring of recycled tropical hardwood.

Opposite, left: An internal lightwell rises through three storeys from a slate-lined pool and decking in a HYLA-designed house in Singapore. *Opposite, right:* In Stefan Schlau's design of Ou Baholyodhin's Bangkok house, the clean geometry of the staircase harmonizes with the scroll motif of the owner's own furniture designs.

and rich colours of hardwood are acceptable only when recycled. The exception is fast-growing teak. Ply-bamboo, too, is rapidly making inroads as a sustainable floor material (see page 63).

An age-old flooring material that has endured is polished cement, a variant on the cocktail of lime, coconut ash, eggshell, coconut milk and oil that was used for the floors of the 16th–18th-century palace of Padmanabhapuram in southern India. In decorative contrast, floor tiles brought by the Dutch to Java may have borne incongruous motifs, but they were eagerly adopted by the wealthy, and Surabaya remains a major production centre. However, it is the cooling effect and muted appearance of slate, terracotta, granite or marble flooring that is now favoured in contemporary Asian houses and that works so well with the dominant natural materials of furnishings.

Chinese and Tibetan carpets are much coveted in the colder northern belt, but have little relevance to the tropical region that is the focus of this book. This is the realm of mats, produced in an infinite variety of textures and colours, from rough coir to finely woven rush and reed or flexible polished bamboo (the latter coming originally from China). And the *tatami*? With its *Edo-ma* (originally for Tokyo houses) modular size of 0.9 x 1.8m (3 x 6ft), this wadded straw-and-rush mat edged by binding has constituted the basic measure for Japanese rooms since the late 15th century. It continues to blossom in a wealth of weaves, patterns and natural tones. Having already survived several thousand years, the mat, the basis of floor-level living, seems unlikely to disappear.

Bamboo

Bamboo balls, a traditional Malay craft item, are
proof of the extreme pliability of bamboo.

Bamboo is the tropical material *par excellence*, unsurpassed in tensile quality, resilience, versatility
and rapid growth. It is transformed into walls, ladders, floors, roof shingles, scaffolding, cooking
utensils, vases, mats, furniture, musical instruments, baskets and even gas and water pipelines. Its
cylindrical form can be split, woven, plaited or used whole; its dense root can be carved into
teapots or sculptures; its young shoots are consumed as a delicacy; and powder extracted from its
secretions is mixed into Chinese medicines. Sticky rice is cooked inside bamboo tubes in Borneo,
umbrellas and bicycles are made from it in Vietnam, and entire houses are constructed from it in
Indonesia, Malaysia and the Philippines. No other plant has such a wealth of applications, inspiring
the Balinese to imbue it with potent, mystical qualities and the Chinese to make it a symbol of
fidelity, humility, wisdom and long life. In more pragmatic terms, bamboo is increasingly regarded as
the magic material for sustainable architecture in the tropics.

A Chinese scientist once calculated that bamboo had 1,386 uses. Such immense versatility,
combined with obvious ecological qualities and its light weight, have resulted in increasing
exploitation. There are over a thousand species of bamboo, although not all are quite as fast-
growing as the Kyoto record-breaker, which shot up 4 feet (121 cm) in twenty-four hours. However,
the inherent pliability of bamboo means that it is earthquake resistant, something stilt-house
dwellers throughout Asia have long appreciated. For decades bamboo has been associated with
poverty and has been overlooked in favour of concrete, but its weight resistance – superior to that
of timber and iron – and its energy-friendly cultivation ought to make it the tropical plant of the
future. Despite any negative connotations, some thirty per cent of Asians still inhabit houses of
bamboo, while the governments of India, China and Burma are now focusing on the economic
benefits of large-scale bamboo production.

China and Japan have always used bamboo for utensils and basketware, and as the basis of lacquerware and furniture. Spotted bamboo in particular was popular for 16th–17th-century Ming chairs and stools. Not only this, Chinese bamboo appeared in the form of prehistoric writing strips before paper was invented in the 2nd–1st centuries BC. It was also used as brush-holders for calligraphers and painters, as well as an essential wrist-rest, so becoming a nurturing element in that ancient culture. At the peak of the colonial era, bamboo's water-resistant qualities resulted in cane furniture and screens becoming classics for use on verandas. After a hiatus, new designs utilizing complex weaves are again flowing from the workshops of Bali, Java and the Philippines, while threaded strips of split bamboo appear in upholstery, mats and blinds.

Rattan (from the Malay *rotan*), a climbing palm with long, jointed stems that grows in tropical forests, is bamboo's only rival. Countless finishing techniques developed for both bamboo and rattan have produced a wide variety of stains and patinas for the export market. With this growing recognition, designers and producers are bringing towel-rails, flexible tablemats of bound strips, woven matting, trays, plant troughs and lampshades to the Western market. Sophisticated flooring techniques, too, are being developed using ply-bamboo, slatted split bamboo or tongue-and-groove, all finished with sealants. It seems that nothing will stop the growth of this environmentally friendly plant.

Above left: A herringbone weave of split bamboo is used by Balinese artisans in this contemporary armchair. *Above centre:* Rolled mats and chickblinds: the bamboo basics. *Above right:* Finely split bamboo has been used to create a checkerboard pattern on this small chest from Lombok.

Living

It may have taken the West until the mid-20th century to discover the benefits of the low occasional table, but in Oriental societies this height has been standard for millennia. The tradition continues in Japan, where standing is viewed as improper, except when moving, and prostrate positions are only for sleeping. As a result, the eye-level of a person seated on the floor is the architecturally dominant perspective in Japan, and is accommodated by low tables and floor cushions. More sensuous is the low-level seating found in many Thai living rooms, where, as in many parts of South-East Asia, the elements are welcomed through generous openings to the exterior. Elsewhere, furniture alternates between Western and Eastern origins: a voluminous Javanese couch of Dutch influence encourages the most indolent reclining; classic Ming yoke-chairs surround a minimalist dining table; or an Italian designer sofa stands beside a cooling, internal pool in Singapore. Yet, whatever the contents of the living room, the key remains the spatial flow between interior and exterior.

CELEBRATING THE ENTRANCE

Guests first experience a house in the entrance hall or lobby, where they are greeted before moving on into the living room. It was the Japanese who developed the symbolic *gengkan*, whose projecting tiled canopy denotes respect and protection for the visitor. While the high threshold from here into the private interior underlines the moment of transition, the *gengkan* also serves a practical purpose as the place where, according to the old Shintoist practice, visitors remove their shoes.

In traditional Chinese communities, the entrance hall is used for displaying the ancestral altar, on which incense is lit daily – a Confucian habit that is still very much alive. Thus, unlike the cramped functional passage common in Western homes, the entrance hall can by some judicious arrangements assume a ceremonial, even spiritual, air. At Mrs Leonora Tan's house in Singapore,

push open the wooden front doors and you are confronted by a large circular carving, a copy of a Cambodian lotus *mandala*, attached to the slate-tiled wall opposite. Concealed uplighting behind symmetrically placed low seats emphasizes the decorative relief, while the wall itself acts like a Chinese spirit wall: visitors move onwards to the right or left but malevolent spirits are stumped. In contrast, the entrance of Nagara's multi-pavilion home in Bangkok offers a complete, enclosed space with three doorways giving a choice of entrance or exit routes. Here, behind two vertical banners flanking a Buddhist sculpture, is a harmonious and aesthetically pleasing space in which to wait. With cushioned benches, bookcases, superlative regional artefacts and views of the garden through openwork carving to enjoy, the guest may well feel no desire to move on.

Equally majestic, if more understated, is the design of the entrance to Sandrine Soimaud's house in Bali. After depositing shoes on the covered walkway outside, the visitor enters a generous space that angles out to become the living and dining area with a veranda and garden beyond. Punctuating this, again in spirit-wall fashion, is a large Javanese chest installed beneath another Javanese import, the *joglo* ceiling system described on page 59. Although discreet, these wooden panels, elevated on slender pillars, accentuate the symbolic step into a private home, while the extended view through full-length windows to distant padi-fields imparts that essential sensation of fluid space. Closer to the Western form is the entrance lobby of the Thai architect Amnad Khitipanna, but even here shoes are left in the good company of superlative antiques, from a Khmer statue to a Ming chair. Again, ceremony and symbolism dominate function.

LIVING THE LIFE

As a social hub for the family and friends, the living room performs an essentially public function. In the East, it assumes an additional, spiritual role. Comfort, harmony and beautiful objects are the classic ingredients everywhere, even in the more restrained traditional style of Japan. Here the focal point is the *tokonoma*, a shelved alcove specifically designed for the selective display of revered objects, *ikebana* (formal flower arrangements) or scroll-paintings. Essentially, because of the absence of Western-style mementos, Japanese rooms become human only through man's presence, but the *tokonoma* is the exception. Significantly, however, the display is not static and objects are regularly substituted from storage chests and trunks.

Typical, too, of many Japanese houses is the *shoin* (study area). Originally a separate room, it later became an elevated window-bay in the reception room. Again, this tradition has been revived in Bangkok by Nagara in his separate study-pavilion overlooking the water garden. Step inside, however, and Japanese associations of serenity are electrified in an assault of colour. In a

Above: Nagara instils a sense of occasion in his entrance pavilion in Bangkok by suspending parallel banners whose iconography echoes the central head of Buddha. Acting like a spirit wall, the banners force circulation to the right or left.

Opposite: The entrance to Sandrine Soimaud's house in Bali is angled outwards and upwards to embrace a living-dining area and padi-field views.

Previous page: Ou Baholyodhin's living room in central Bangkok, viewed here from the mezzanine bedroom, overlooks a pool area through glazed sliding doors. The interior mixes Baholyodhin's own furniture designs for Jim Thompson with local ceramics and artefacts.

contemporary painting depicting a stylized sun and waves, a luminous palette of oranges is reflected in gold and red lacquerware on the desk.

The classic Japanese reception room is a place of metamorphosis, and its relatively large scale (a minimum of eight *tatami* mats) means it can readily be transformed into a dining room or a temporary sleeping area for an honoured guest. Low tables and floor cushions are the rule. This is also the norm in Thailand, with the addition of a triangle of cylindrical cushions to provide back support. The graphic forms and rich hues of Thai and Burmese lacquered food stands, as in Thai designer Ou Baholyodhin's guest apartment in Bangkok, complete the sense of visual and sensual comfort.

GOD IS IN THE DECORATIVE DETAIL

Carved Thai furniture creates instant sumptuousness in an interior and mixes successfully with the visual complexity of Chinese, Burmese or Thai lacquerware. Craftsmen in both Bali and Bangkok are skilled at copying old designs, and cabriole table legs made only yesterday echo more authentic antique curves elsewhere. They also impart an unmistakably Oriental accent: even the 14th-century Japanese *bundai* (low calligrapher's table) with its outward-turning ends stood on such inward-turned legs. Curves reach their extreme in Javanese couches or benches that were strongly influenced by Dutch colonial tastes of the late 18th century; with a quasi-Biedermeier elegance, they often

Above left: Compressed and polished coconut shell, made in Java, is used for counters and side tables at the Begawan Giri. *Above centre:* Contemporary Thai products include gilded coconut shells and matt black ceramic bowls, a teak table-stand on a teak coffee table with opaque glass top, and hemp cushions layered in silk and organza. All are designed by Cocoon, Bangkok. *Above right:* Visitors entering this house in Singapore are faced by a spirit wall displaying a handcarved Cambodian lotus *mandala* (the Buddhist emblem of truth and purity) behind symmetrically placed seats.

Opposite: Dazzling colour in a contemporary Thai painting dominates Nagara's study-pavilion. Celadon vases, lacquered boxes and copies of classical Ming furniture enhance the Oriental flavour.

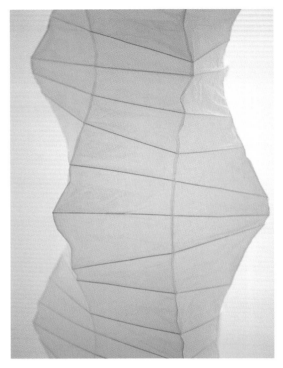

Above left: A floor lamp in brilliant orange raw silk designed by Ou Baholyodhin is set against a plum-red wall, thereby creating a vivid corner of colour in an otherwise pure white space. *Above right:* Noguchi's 1950s classic: the sinuous curves of his Akari lamp impart a glowing luminosity.

Opposite: A contemporary interpretation of traditional Asian features has been brilliantly executed by architects SCDA at the Teng house in Singapore. The use of changing levels (of honed siltstone), glimpses of the upper floor and exterior, and the integration of gravel-lined pools produces a clear sensation of fluid space.

incorporate caning. These designs are still made today and appear in homes from Jakarta to Bali or Singapore, sometimes with a twist – at Linda Garland's house the upholstery is finely woven rattan.

More in tune with today's minimalist tastes is the furniture created by Ou Baholyodhin in Thailand. These coffee tables, consoles and side tables in solid dark teak, although designed for Western lifestyles, bear the unmistakable imprint of the Chinese in a subtle, geometrical expression of the scroll motif at the base. Again, it is traditional Japanese ingenuity that produced a form that still works today: the *kotatsu*, a low, rectangular table with a heater located inside its smaller base. Less refined, though perfectly adapted to the climate and the open-sided rooms of Bali, are outsized chairs and sofas of bamboo that invite mountains of cushions in local fabrics. Storage and display furniture varies from glass-fronted Sumatran cabinets, again with colonial Dutch origins, to Chinese polished or lacquered wooden cupboards or a Qing dynasty composite arrangement of seventeen wooden cases of different sizes that fit together. Equally inventive is the Japanese *kaidan-dansu*, a composite of stepped cupboards and drawers designed to go under a staircase. But storage is an ongoing issue, and drawers now also appear in such unexpected places as the side of a Thai mirror frame, in the base of a Javanese couch or in the solid wooden frame of a 1980s armchair designed by Shiro Kuramata.

The materials currently used in contemporary Asian living areas may have been around for a long time, but their textural qualities and modern treatments propel them straight into the tastes of the

21st century. Yellow jackwood (an old favourite for Vietnamese sculpture), dark brown speckled coconut-palm wood, black bamboo, mangowood and coconut shell all become smoothly contemporary surfaces. Meanwhile, copies of antique bronze Burmese or Thai drums make decorative occasional tables or stools, as do Chinese barrel-shaped ceramic or wooden stools, both types being highlighted with decorative detailing. It was the Japanese Sori Yanagi, however, who designed perhaps the most ethereal stool yet: his winged 'butterfly' stool dates from 1956 but fits any contemporary interior.

COLOUR AND LIGHT

The Chinese loved colour and applied it in several ways. For contrast, warm tones were juxtaposed with cool, one colour with its complementary (for example, red and green), or black with white (both being counted as primary colours); for harmony, colours adjacent on the colour wheel were used (for example, red, orange and yellow). Shades of jade green (jade is the Chinese symbol of the perfection of human virtue) characterized the glaze of roof tiles and porcelain. But if one colour symbolizes the Orient, it is red. Be it cinnabar red, vermilion, copper red or crimson, it is universally applied to walls, pillars, food stands, furniture, ceramics and textiles. When combined with gold, this symbol of joy, the south, and the yang principle can be sumptuously rich or discreetly refined; all depends on balance and structure.

Above: Sliding glazed walls draw the eye towards the landscape beyond in this Japanese teahouse. The minimal furnishings of floor cushions and choice *objets d'art* help to focus the visual flow.

Opposite: The rich tones and stylized motifs of this Chinese lacquered screen set off the beauty of a rare Burmese Buddhist sculpture at Amnad Khitipanna's Bangkok home.

1

2

Storage systems in Asia are as ingenious as they are decorative. *(1)* A 19th-century Chinese four-door openwork cabinet preserves its original polychrome lacquer. *(2)* A Korean copy of a Japanese *kaidan dansu* (staircase cupboard) at Kristina Zanic's Bangkok house doubles as a storage system and display area for a rare collection of 19th-century Chinese opera figures. *(3)* In the same house, a Thai elephant chair stands in front of an 18th-century Chinese cupboard in matt lacquer. The scarf is of Vietnamese silk. *(4)* Drawers in the base of a semi-gilded Balinese bench at the Puri Anyar Krambitan store precious Benares silks.

3

4

1

2

3

4

Variations on the art of reclining. *(1)* The living area of the Begawan Giri's Tirta-Ening pavilion, which stands open to a garden of frangipani trees, water channels and bamboo. The furniture mixes Javanese with Chinese styles. *(2)* The treetop views of this corner of Kathy Kamei's lofty living room are emphasized by the diagonal placing of an elegant Balinese bench. The bamboo armchair and versatile stools, used here as a coffee table, are also locally made. *(3)* A curtained recess at Linda Garland's estate in Bali creates a secluded corner where guests can recline on a Javanese couch upholstered in finely woven rattan. *(4)* Relaxed living with nature in a Singapore suburb, where a planter's chair reclines beneath a bamboo awning.

Regal Javanese splendour marries the tropical elements in the Begawan Giri's Umabona royal suite. Polished hardwood floors reflect Burmese lacquerware and Javanese brass utensils, and form a stage for carved Javanese wood panels and cane-backed benches.

Today, contemporary Asian homes are dominated by the harmonious, muted palette of natural materials. The predominance of subtle vegetable dyes means this barely alters, even in multicoloured, traditional batik, ikat and Japanese indigo textiles. Exceptions come in the Balinese use of red and gold, in the glittering silk *songket* (brocades) of Malaysia and Indonesia, and in increasingly inventive Thai cushions where double layers of organza and silk create ever varying shades.

If the otherwise restful uniformity of a living room is offset by flashes of colour, these are found in lacquerware, gilded items, lamps or contemporary monochrome upholstery. Indian coloured glass

lamps and Chinese paper lanterns will dynamize an interior from above, while Ou Baholyodhin's rectangular floor lamps, in their varied hues of vivid Thai silk, vitalize dominant neutrals. In contrast, Isamu Noguchi's sculptural Akari lamps, designed in the early 1950s and now much-imitated design classics, rely not on colour but on luminous whiteness for effect (the word *akari* means the essence of lightness). Made of the same *washi* (mulberry bark paper) as traditional *shoji* screens, they bring a lunar glow to the interior.

Fearlessness in the application of colour is demonstrated by Bill Bensley, a Bangkok-based designer of interiors and landscapes. He will paint a shuttered, internal window frame in the same

1

2

3

4

Pockets of decorative detailing. *(1)* A beautifully carved Chinese Qing dynasty chair highlighted by a vivid orange silk cushion at Amnad Khitipanna's Bangkok house. *(2)* A shuttered internal window at Bill Bensley's house in Bangkok, decorated by Jirachai Rengthong to complement a remodelled Burmese bench, Thai silk cushions, a framed Sumatran weaving and a collection of Asian teapots. *(3)* Kathy Kamei's Japanese connections, which bring an informal low-level *tatami* and floor-cushion area into a corner of the luminous living room. *(4)* A room within a room created in the Walter Spies suite at the Tugu Hotel, Bali. By inserting a carved wooden panel on a low wall behind a sofa, the study area is clearly defined and yet easily accessible.

Opposite: Martin Smyth's design of the living room at the Villa Melati is based on a traditional Balinese pavilion. Only chickblinds act as a barrier to the sun and rain. Exclusive use of natural materials includes terracotta floor tiles, woven bamboo floor cushions and coconutwood columns. The benches and table are from Java and Madura.

Above: Communicating areas create a sense of fluid space as in this Tugu Hotel suite, where a carved and mirrored Javanese bed harmonizes with the couch of the sitting area. Ikat cushion covers and upholstery add warm, earthy tones.

Opposite: In Ou Baholyodhin's guest apartment in Bangkok, folding Thai floor cushions in brilliant hues of silk lie beside Burmese and northern Thai lacquerware, Thai basketware, Chinese lions and a Burmese temple statue. The panelled wardrobe doors were copied from Chinese designs.

oranges and turquoises as the silk cushions that are piled on a couch in the living room beyond, or, not without humour, will gild the interior of a cupboard.

Firmly entrenched in Eastern mythology, gold is number one in feng shui's five elements, as well as being the object of the ancient Taoists' alchemical claims. For gold is light: apply it to virtually any surface and a rich, reflective effect is created. If gilded, the interior of a simple coconut shell imparts such luminosity that it appears to contain a light source: a paradoxical combination of low- and high-life materials. The use of gold for visual impact has been taken to excess by the Balinese, whereas the Japanese, ever restrained, merely sprinkle their lacquerware with gold powder. Subtle gilding, however, was evidently not the case with this 13th-century palace in Japan described from hearsay by Marco Polo: 'The entire roof is covered with a plating of gold … The ceilings of the halls are of the same precious metal; many of the apartments have small tables of pure gold … and the windows also have golden ornaments.'

Lacquer

Criticized by early Confucian writers as *yinqiao*, a worldly distraction, lacquer is undoubtedly the most overtly luxurious of Oriental crafts. Its attraction seems unlikely to fade, however morally corrupting it may be deemed.

The richness and depth of lacquer's lustrous surface has been prized by the upper echelons of Far Eastern society since prehistoric times. As early as 80 BC, a Han dynasty writer estimated that a piece of lacquerware cost ten times as much to produce as an item of bronze. The cost derived from its labour-intensive production: the best-quality lacquerwork took well over two years to produce, with a lengthy process of base-making being followed by the application of up to a hundred coats of lacquer (two hundred for carved lacquer), each requiring a week to dry. Today this is practised only in Wajima, Japan, the country where lacquer was once applied in boats at sea so that not one speck of dust could intervene. China first held the monopoly on lacquer products, partly owing to the easy availability of the basic resin, but also because it developed large, organized workforces.

Used on bamboo, wood, cloth (wrapped around a model that was subsequently removed to leave a stiffened outer form) or even camel hide, this impermeable coating would be progressively coloured, inlaid, carved or painted, and then ground and polished. Classic lacquer base colours are black and cinnabar red. These may be inlaid with gold, silver or mother-of-pearl, the latter being a favourite in Korea, Thailand and Myanmar. Under the Ming dynasty (1368–1644), polychrome carved lacquer reached its apotheosis at the same time as numerous other decorative techniques were being developed in Japan. Here, beauty remained surface deep and true to the soul of the material, since Japanese techniques such as *makie* (sprinkling or mixing in powdered gold or silver) never affected the smooth surface and the gloss.

The ridged, sculptural forms of red ochre and black lacquered *hsun-ok* (offering vessels) from Myanmar are composed of layered offering trays.

Decorative yet resilient, lightweight and, above all, easily packed, lacquerware has always been a profitable export to the West. Tastes, however, have changed since the days when gold motifs of peonies, mountains, dragons and pagodas would blanket the surface of tea caddies, desks, screens, chairs or sewing tables in European drawing rooms. In a return to 13th-century Yuan dynasty styles, today's preference is for intense monochromes, including gold and silver, with little or no decoration. Yet because of the mushrooming of low-price, mass-produced synthetic finishes in Vietnam, the main producer of lacquerware outside Japan, very few of these items are now made in the original time-honoured and time-intensive way.

The lacquerware that is produced with a matt, cinnabar or black finish for daily use in Thailand and Myanmar is of a different quality: its beauty lies in sculptural form rather than in a mirror-like surface. Even when some of the surface lacquer wears away with use, these pieces possess an intrinsic and very pure beauty. A lacquered item much collected for its striking three-dimensional form is the Burmese *hsun-ok*. This is composed of superimposed offering trays culminating in an inverted cup or spike. Monochrome bowls and food stands as well as lacquered containers and basketware are common throughout Myanmar, northern Thailand, southern Sumatra and parts of China.

Above left: These 19th-century Chinese lacquered finger-bowls, delicately painted with goldfish on a muted gold background, stand on a contemporary Vietnamese lacquered tray. *Above centre:* Chinese pigskin- or vellum-covered camphorwood trunks are usually painted with protective layers of lacquer. *Above right:* Black and gold lacquer tea-bowls, made in Vietnam for Asian Motifs, Bangkok, reflect contemporary tastes for monochrome lacquerware and purist forms.

Eating

Food and its preparation are essential elements in man's physical and mental well-being, and Asia stands at the forefront of culinary complexities. Rituals and customs in the manner both of cooking and of consumption encompass numerous regional and social variations. While mat-level eating continues to be the norm in Japan and in stilt-houses throughout rural South-East Asia, elsewhere the Chinese wok imposes specific cooking conditions. Above all, the widespread use of staff (perhaps not quite the 9,462 servants who toiled in the palace kitchens under the Ming dynasty) in wealthy Asian homes means that this section of the house is not always nurtured as much as others.

Although Western-style kitchens and dining tables, varying in sophistication according to social level, have become the rule in urban societies, tried and tested eating habits die hard and utensils follow suit. Asia's staple food, rice, was cultivated from about 5000 BC in southern China, from where it swept across South-East Asia. Now rice is usually cooked in the ubiquitous electric steamer. Much more visually seductive, however, are traditional ceramic noodle bowls, wooden chopsticks, lacquered food stands or square, terracotta teapots with tiny cups – just some of the enduring forms that have also won Westerners over.

KITCHEN STYLES

Typical of many Chinese homes is the outdoor kitchen. With the pungent odours that emanate from a wok and the fast and furious flames of the burner itself, this is far more suitable than the Western-style, indoor kitchen. Many modern Singaporean townhouses still incorporate the outdoor kitchen at the back of the house, in a roofed veranda protected from the elements by a classic chickblind. In traditional urban houses of China, rudimentary kitchens were adjacent to an internal courtyard or

lightwell for obvious ventilation purposes, a practice that was passed on to Vietnam and the Peranakan communities of Singapore and Malaysia. In the *siheyuan* (courtyard houses of northern China) food preparation would take place in and outside the servants' quarters at the front of the courtyard. In contrast, each family unit of a communal Borneo longhouse has its own kitchen area at the back of the multi-purpose family room. Cooking smells disappear rapidly through the bamboo walls, while smoke from the fire has a convenient preservative effect on the thatched *attap* roof. This, too, is where the family eats its meals, seated on mats, although the drying of grains and some food preparation takes place on the unroofed platform outside or in the intermediate *ruai*, a roofed corridor.

Western-style kitchens are often connected in open-plan style to the dining and living areas. Epitomizing this formula are the Balinese houses of Kathy Kamei and John Taylor, both of which have storage units functioning as serving places and barriers between the cooking area and the entertaining spaces. At Kathy Kamei's house, an additional ironwork structure creates shelving and hanging space for frequently used implements without blocking the visual flow, while the cupboards below it are accessible from both the kitchen and dining sides. Hot, humid conditions and the prolific use of vegetables and fruit have inspired the utilization of wicker baskets as drawers, allowing produce to breathe while being concealed from view and light.

Above left: A wrought-iron structure set above a cupboard unit creates a functional room divider between kitchen and dining area at Kathy Kamei's Balinese home. *Above centre:* Sliding wicker baskets allow produce to breathe. *Above right:* Nothing is hidden in Linda Garland's kitchen: utensils are easily accessible on open shelving units.

Opposite: White on pristine white: panelled wood units and stools create a restful kitchen at Kristina Zanic's house in Bangkok. The only colour to enter the picture is the framed Thai hilltribe embroidery.

Previous page: Eating becomes almost ceremonial in Nagara's Bangkok house, where diners mingle with superlative Thai antiques. Garden views through glazed doors create a Japanese mood, while China is represented in copies of classical Ming chairs, the lacquered foodstand and porcelain from Beijing.

Lunching with nature in the raised pavilion at
Carole Muller's Balinese home. Coconut-palm
wood platters by Emily Readett-Bailey stand beside
Chinese bowls on the table. The hoop-backed
Balinese chairs are of varnished rattan.

In Kristina Zanic's Bangkok house the kitchen is even more completely open to view from
the dining area. The latter is a section of the large living room, which, in turn, opens through
full-length glazed doors onto the veranda and garden. In the purist universe of the kitchen,
uniformly white, panelled cupboards keeping utensils and ingredients invisible are matched by
a freestanding unit that acts as serving counter and breakfast bar. The only hint of colour comes
from framed hilltribe textiles and a discreet alcove displaying a collection of rare prehistoric
pottery from Ban Chiang and Lopburi. While the subtle, natural pigments of the ancient
vessels harmonize with the ambient whiteness, their original culinary functions reflect the
kitchen environment.

More immediately functional is Carole Muller's kitchen, where she or her cook works with ingredients and utensils that are visible and to hand. When the Balinese staff come on duty, they bring with them tiny rice and banana-leaf offerings to the various kitchen gods. More permanent Oriental touches come in the form of Japanese paper lamps and Chinese rice bowls and, less obviously, in the method of construction of the shelving: made using Balinese principles of wedges and dowels, it can be completely dismantled. Through a beaded curtain lies an outdoor kitchen-cum-scullery and, beyond, an open dining area where Carole hosts 'moon-viewing' dinners amidst a riot of lush, fragrant vegetation. Shady lunches are taken on the raised terrace of a *bale* (pavilion) with views over the neighbouring water palace, while the front veranda of the main structure is

Above: By framing the landscape of Balinese padi-fields with carved Javanese panels, Sandrine Soimaud creates an instant still life. The lacquerware containers and food stand are from Sumatra, while the compartmentalized box is for betel ingredients.

used for lingering breakfasts. This multiplicity of eating areas encapsulates the versatility of Asian living, an aspect to which most contemporary Balinese houses aspire.

DINING IN SPLENDOUR

Traditional Balinese compounds for those of high social status have separate pavilions for serving large meals to honoured guests. The 17th-century Puri Anyar, a palace compound in Krambitan inhabited by five related families, typifies this custom with a long table that accommodates an array of food stands as well as twenty or so diners. Contemporary Balinese design enters the equation in the form of folding teak chairs whose simple lines are in complete contrast to the elaborately gilded details of the pavilion structure. This style of pavilion dining has been revived on a more intimate scale at the Puri Merta hotel where, instead of going to a central restaurant, hotel guests are served meals in their private *bale*, just a few steps from the veranda and bedroom. Again, spatial flow rules.

By incorporating traditional features, contemporary dining and cooking areas in Asia evoke their cultural origins without sacrificing any of the functionality gained through technology. One of Sandrine Soimaud's dining rooms in her Balinese house is entirely furnished with Javanese panelling and furniture and, while the framed view of padi-fields is inimitably Balinese, behind the

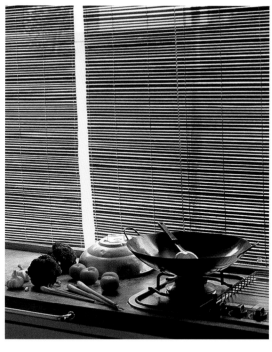

1

2

3

4

Despite obvious Western influence in eating habits, certain Asian traditions remain deeply anchored, from outdoor kitchens to crackleglaze tableware. *(1)* Essential to every Chinese home is the outdoor kitchen, designed to cope with wok flames and aromas. Chickblinds act as shields against sun and rain. *(2)* Checkerboard banana-fibre mats contrast with speckled ceramic plates, both from Bali, on Kathy Kamei's dining table. *(3)* A sober line-up of 19th-century Chinese ceramic bowls on Ou Baholyodhin's teak dining table in Bangkok, featuring crackleware and deep emerald glazes. *(4)* The kitchen in Carole Muller's Bali house allies practicality with Oriental accents, such as Chinese lamps and bowls, and shelving that, in the Balinese tradition, can be dismantled.

carved doors lies a completely Westernized kitchen. Even more Oriental in reference is Nagara's shadowy dining pavilion in Bangkok, where a Chinese dining table and chairs are surrounded by glittering Thai artworks. Eating here is no mere function: it allows time to absorb the beauty of surrounding *objets d'art*, which include shelves of Chinese porcelain installed in front of a glazed wall. And, concealed behind a teakwood partition only a few paces away, with access to an outdoor area, is the kitchen.

IMPLEMENTS FOR NOURISHMENT

The spectrum of Asian food-related implements is immense, ranging from miniature works of art in ceramic or wood that are in fact chopstick stands to Japanese *bento*-boxes (compartmentalized lunchboxes), enamelled Chinese basins, coconut-shell serving spoons, lacquered trays, solid ceramic storage jars and crackleglaze porcelain bowls. From high level to low, one thing is certain: food in the Orient is a daily, much respected feast. Complex, time-consuming preparation has resulted in the development of specialist utensils that the West has only recently learned to appreciate, notably the wok and the stacked bamboo steamer. The same skills that have produced exquisite porcelain and lacquerware for thousands of years continue today, and craft manufacturing centres such as Bali, Bangkok and Saga (Japan) excel at adapting to changing tastes in both West and East. Placemats, an example of East–West fusion, now exist in a dazzling variety of natural fibres and patterns, ranging from Filipino *abaca* (a semi-rigid fabric made from a relative of the banana palm) to woven or split bamboo, loose-weave pineapple fibre or ikat textiles. The Philippines, Thailand, India and Indonesia dominate this field.

TEA RITUALS

The teapot is a utensil that has produced a wealth of forms, in tune with the importance placed upon, and ritualistic manner of, tea-drinking in the Far East. According to an old Japanese proverb, 'If man has no tea in him he is incapable of understanding truth and beauty.' This attitude has resulted in extraordinary attention to the quality and form of teabowls and cups, as these are the elements that touch the lips of the drinker.

Although the brew itself (*ch'a*) originated in prehistoric China, becoming popularized during the Tang dynasty (618–907), it was the Japanese who elevated it to a ritual within the context of Zen Buddhism. *Cha-no-yu*, the Zen tea ceremony, led to the existence of separate tearooms where participants, limited to the symbolic number of five, were grouped on *tatami* mats around a low table. From the early 17th century, this tradition spread from the upper classes to all strata of

Above: Dressed for a feast, the Puri Anyar's dining table combines red and gold tablecloths and 300-year-old architectural features with contemporary teak folding chairs.

Opposite: This perspective of the dining room at Villa Melati, Bali, leads the eye through glazed sliding doors to a cantilevered deck with plunging views over the Ayung gorge. Merbau wood diagonals dynamize the terracotta tiles, the Balinese dining table is newly fabricated from old teakwood, and the chairs are Javanese. Out of view to the right is a serving counter and the kitchen.

Above left: A traditional Japanese teapot made of mud fired in a *tazimi* kiln, plus teabowl and tray, all from Kara-Kara, London. *Above right:* A raised bed-tray with Thai teapot and ovoid ceramic beakers stands on a couch reworked from an elephant howdah.

Opposite: Veranda dining at Sandrine Soimaud's Balinese house. The open-sided Javanese day bed draped with a Klungklung ikat faces an assortment of Javanese chairs and the boldly coloured bands of a tablecloth from Lombok, designed by Marie Verlant.

Japanese society. In Vietnam, too, custom dictates that when strangers meet it is over a pot of tea sipped in repeated thimbleful doses. Buddhist Korea shares the custom, while on the opposite side of Asia the entire Indian subcontinent is addicted to sweet, milky *chai* traditionally drunk out of tiny, disposable, terracotta bowls.

Cups, beakers and teapots are smaller than the Western equivalent, often made with rough glazes or in simple clay, whose porous quality encourages tea leaves to release their flavour. It was when powdered tea gave way to loose leaves in the Yuan dynasty (1271–1368) that teabowls were gradually replaced by teapots and teacups, chiefly in brown stoneware. These were exported to Japan, where other materials such as cast iron came to be used for teapots. Ceramic or porcelain, the material traditionally favoured for Chinese teabowls, became more common when the tea-drinking habit migrated to Europe in the 17th century and stimulated a multiplicity of exportware designs. A constantly bubbling metal ewer or kettle also enters the picture, as green or black tea is repeatedly rebrewed. However, the ultimate example of tea-related refinement is perhaps the black ceramic bowl of the Song dynasty (960–1279), much favoured for the aesthetic contrast it provided with the white froth of the whipped tea.

Ceramics

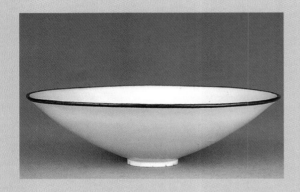

The purity of this 12th-century Dingware porcelain bowl exemplifies the unsurpassed refinement of Song dynasty Chinese techniques.

Take a globular, 'full-moon' jar from Korea, a jade-green altar stemcup from China's imperial Longquan kilns or a prehistoric handpainted Ban Chiang pot from Thailand, and you are faced with extremes. For Asian pottery goes back some 8,000 years and it is hardly surprising that techniques, forms and decorative styles are so varied. From their origin in China, ceramic techniques spread to neighbouring Thailand, Vietnam, Korea and Japan, while the Silk Road brought Indian and Persian influences. In Asia today, it is Japan, Vietnam and Thailand that are the most innovative producers.

In harmony with 21st-century minimalist interiors, contemporary taste gravitates towards monochrome ceramics. At the very most, decoration consists of the crackled effect produced when the glaze shrinks more than the underlying clay during the final stages of cooling. Yet the use of a single colour is nothing new, for during China's Song dynasty (960–1279), when the first high-quality glazed porcelain was produced by organized mass-manufacture, luminous imperial yellow, ivory white, celadon or copper red dominated the market. A Song dynasty celadon, Guan ware, is considered to be the first example of the still-popular crackleglaze.

Contemporaneously, porcelain of similar quality was being produced in the Red River delta of Vietnam, where roof tiles, bricks and functional items assumed monochrome white, jade-green or brown glazes. Parallel to this, Korea's Koryo dynasty (918–1392) excelled in beautifully turned and glazed celadon and whiteware whose stylistic restraint stemmed from strict Confucianism. In contrast, Japanese ceramics of the period remained undeveloped, with unglazed grey or reddish-black pottery being the norm. More refined tastes were catered for by Vietnamese, Korean and Chinese imports until the late 16th century, when emigrant Korean potters laid the foundations of Japan's porcelain industry, above all at Arita. The newly established vogue of the tea ceremony encouraged a plethora of polychrome glazes, motifs and forms alongside Chinese and Korean

derivatives. From then on, during Japan's 250-year period of self-isolation, production was much influenced by European baroque and rococo fashions, which filtered through its one licensed trader, the Dutch East India Company.

The high point of Thai and Vietnamese ceramics came in the 14th–16th centuries, when these goods flooded the markets of South-East Asia during the Ming ban on sea trade. However, Chinese resurgence brought with it a new model: the infinitely varied blue-and-white porcelain that rapidly conquered the West. The introduction of cobalt blue to Vietnam inspired the blue-and-white ceramics of Hue, while Japan and Thailand both readily adopted this highly decorative style. For the Chinese themselves, blue-and-white became standard tableware for those unable to afford gold and silver. Ming porcelain still dominates the collectors' market, closely followed by Qing *famille verte* and *famille rose* (enamel-decorated porcelains) made from the Kangxi period (1662–1722) onwards.

East–West fusion in ceramics may have first blossomed in the exportware designed for European markets during the 17th–19th centuries, but it continues apace today. Japanese products complement Western tastes in the matt surfaces of fine biscuitware (low-fired, unglazed ceramics) and tougher stoneware, as well as in elegant forms of refined white or celadon porcelain. Not least, Thailand's ceramic designers excel in creating non-traditional, densely coloured glazes and new designs that are completely attuned to global tastes.

Above left: Simple white noodle-soup bowls from Cocoon, Bangkok. *Above centre:* Square stoneware plates contrast with silver chopsticks, both examples of Japanese design adapted to Western tastes. *Above right:* These Celadon plates, bowls and food stands are engraved with motifs derived from Thai hilltribe textiles. A design by Asian Motifs, Bangkok.

Bathing

Water – and its associations with cleanliness – is a basic human need, much accentuated in the East by its ready abundance. Monsoon rains, natural springs and coursing rivers, not to mention the tens of thousands of islands surrounded by sea, are integral to the landscape. For many Asians, cleansing the body is far from a daily chore and attains the status of a regenerative ritual, extending its reach to the mind and consequently the soul. At its most extreme, ritualized cleansing is practised by millions of Indians, who bathe in the polluted Ganges to purify their sins – though perhaps not their body.

Affinity with and respect for water has produced countless variations on the practice of ablutions – all very different from Western urban societies, where water is merely the product of a tap. For centuries, massage rooms and freshwater pools were integrated into the homes of prosperous southern Indians but, while most rural Asians were using a bucket and well, it was the Japanese who first gave substantial space, time and importance to the bathroom. If the development of furniture was very much a Chinese prerogative, bathing has long been that of these masters of the ablutionary art. Follow their example and bathing can generate a sense of repose that, if combined with a massage, leads to a state of being close to nirvana. In more energetic mode, outdoor showers – the original 'wet' bathroom – allow you to commune with nature and, on a more practical level, to dispense with curtains, partitions and elaborate drainage systems.

JAPANESE SCRUBS AND SOAKS

While river-bathing is still the norm in many parts of rural Asia, in Japan the spa traditions run deep – which is hardly surprising in a country with around 20,000 hot-water springs of volcanic origin. An entire culture has grown up around these *onsen* (communal bath-houses) and *roten buro* (open-air baths), extending to massages and integrated teahouses. In the private family domain,

houses first used the *gonemburo*, a gigantic cast-iron cauldron that was heated directly over the fire. *Ofuro*, rectangular, semi-lidded bathtubs of aromatic cypresswood, later became the norm and this clean, minimalist form endures today in some Western-style bathrooms in Tokyo and Osaka.

Shorter and deeper than classic Western bathtubs, Japanese tubs allow the seated bather to soak in shoulder-high water behind planks that prevent the water cooling. Bathing traditionally took place in order of rank, starting with the head of the family, followed by other males and then the female members of the family. This system no longer operates, but the tub is still large enough to allow children to bathe with a parent. This sharing of water is far from unhygienic as it is actually the second, contemplative stage in the cleansing ritual: before plunging into the tub, the bather undergoes a soapy scour using a body brush or glove and then rinses off with a hand-shower or with water ladled from a small barrel. This double bathing technique is perhaps the ultimate sign of respect for the purifying qualities of water.

Originally separate from the main living pavilion, though connected by a corridor or veranda, the Japanese bathroom was later brought adjacent to the kitchen for practical purposes. The traditional sense of *wabi* (respecting the essence of a material) reappears in the natural materials used – chiefly wood, stone and bamboo – and, true to form, an attempt is always made to integrate the natural world outside. While ceramic tiles and fibreglass tubs are fast replacing traditional items on the home ground, Japanese bathing implements and slatted wooden decks are creeping into Western bathrooms. The square form of the bathtub itself has been reinterpreted by contemporary architects in cast concrete, marble and even wood. Will bamboo waterpipes come next?

OUTDOOR BATHING

A comparable incorporation of nature into the washing experience has been pioneered by ground-breaking hotels in Bali. Over the last two decades, outdoor bathrooms have emerged from curtains of dense tropical foliage, a practice that countless private houses rapidly imitated. Similar styles have since appeared in hotels of southern India, Sri Lanka, Malaysia and Thailand, where traditional habits are adapted to Western tastes for the 'exotic'. You can soak in a moonlit tub while breathing in the fragrance of frangipani and being hammered by tropical rain; watch a palpitating golden frog as you brush your teeth in tune with the cicada symphony of the night air; or awake to an invigorating shower on an open deck in front of a waterfall. Washing becomes a sensual pleasure in tune with the elements, not just a necessary task.

Outdoor and semi-outdoor bathrooms are now a true Balinese design form, ranging from the rustic thatch-and-bamboo style of Linda Garland to more sophisticated hybrids where an antique

Opposite: Limewashed doors are built into a polished cement basin unit in Sandrine Soimaud's master bathroom. To the right is a walled patio replete with plants. Added refinement comes from a pair of antique Javanese mirrors and a carved, mythical elephant head from a Burmese temple.

Previous page: The ultimate bathroom for Oriental ablutions at the Begawan Giri: symmetrically placed carved doors at either end echo the central shutters above the bath, so allowing an open or closed bathing universe. The buffalo-hide lamps are by Melbourne designer Nathan Thompson.

carving, a dresser and a mirror stand next to a clump of papyrus or a lotus pond, as at Sandrine Soimaud's house. When pebbles and wooden decking are used inside a sliding glass wall that opens onto a verdant walled patio, as designed by Martin Smyth, tactile and visual sensations clearly reflect the classic Japanese aesthetic. More extreme in form, Kathy Kamei's guest bathroom is a perfect example of the tropical 'wet' bathroom. The shower section, open to the skies, is backed by a bamboo wall with a rectangular opening overlooking the garden, while water simply drains away between the wooden floorboards.

Walls may be partially or totally absent, depending on the privacy of the property. The most striking neo-modernist example of a bathroom with no walls at all is, yet again, to be found in Japan in Shigeru Ban's Villa Kuru in Nagano. Here, one whole side of this hillside villa embraces nature in a generous, open, white space protected only by the roof. Both the bathtub and WC stand on the edge of this purist universe, cooled by the sea breeze and aromatically and visually enveloped by a forest of pines.

Even when walls are present, nature can still be integrated into the room, as in a bathroom at the Begawan Giri hotel in Bali. Here, the focus is on monumental carved doors that swing open onto verdant terraces, their form repeated in shutters above the bath itself. Although it is not quite an outdoor bathroom, there is an exquisite balance between the untamed beauty of the exterior and

Left: Simple open shelving beneath a thatched roof encloses an outdoor washing area at the Linda Garland estate. An assortment of Indonesian artefacts raises the area above the merely utilitarian and rustic.

Opposite: Anyone showering on this deck at Linda Garland's Balinese estate achieves a sense of oneness with the waterfall that streams down the hillside opposite. Huge terracotta pots enhance the natural surroundings.

1

2

Water containers vary from traditional jars to Western-influenced basins with a twist. *(1)* A gigantic water jar strewn with frangipani blossoms makes a refined version of a *mandi* (Indonesian wash tank) at Bali's Puri Merta. *(2)* In Bangkok, Bill Bensley has plumbed a Thai hardwood bowl and lined it with pebbles in a fresh take on a Western-style basin. The copper tap was custom made, while the antique bronze bell behind is from Nepal. *(3)* Semi-outdoor bathing at the Tugu Hotel, Bali, where a jacuzzi tub is backed up by a water jar and ladle. *(4)* A stone basin in Kathy Kamei's guest bathroom, seen in photograph *(2)*, opposite.

3

4

1

2

3

4

Bali remains king of imaginative outdoor bathroom design. *(1)* Papyrus and bamboo in a bathroom at Villa Sawah are reflected in a carved Javanese mirror above the polished cement bathtub. *(2)*, The bamboo walls, floor and towel rail are the main features of this simple yet functional bathroom at Kathy Kamei's house. *(3)* A small, verdant patio at Carole Muller's house features a full-size statue of the god Vishnu plumbed in to provide a footbath, *mandi* or shower. *(4)* Outside a pavilion bedroom at the Puri Merta hotel, a partitioned overhang shields the shower, basin and WC area. From here flagstones lead across a pebbled garden to the sunken tub.

man's refinement of the structure. In the individually walled garden-bathrooms of the Puri Merta hotel in Bali, the shower, basin and WC are located beneath projecting eaves to offer a view over the private garden and its focal point: a stone bathtub embedded in the ground. Either way, tropical rains are catered for. Again, the exterior steps inside and, again, it is only the roof that remains and the constant warmth of the climate that rules.

Improvized recycling is often the key to attuning bathroom accessories to the exterior: the stumps of branches on a propped-up bough can become hooks for bathrobes; a bamboo ladder can be used for slinging towels; a wooden bowl partly filled with pebbles acts as a plumbed basin. Bamboo reappears in towel rails, so lightweight that they can be shifted around according to need. A less portable though ubiquitous bathroom component is the stone or ceramic water jar and ladle, the traditional washing tools of South-East Asia. Indonesian bathing, when not in the river, centres on the *mandi*, a large tank of water from which the bather ladles water over his soaped body in the same way as the Japanese pre-soak wash. Revealing her stylistic wit, Carole Muller, a confessed *mandi* addict, has plumbed a lifesize statue of Vishnu to fill her patio water-container, installed a Japanese-style, stone lantern in the adjacent vegetation and hung a transparent plastic curtain to prevent exuberant splashes inside the house. The combination of these elements thus turns a morning wash into a multicultural experience. At

Above left: Another view of the Begawan Giri bathroom featured on pages 98–99 shows side doors opening onto the terrace, an antique ironwood and rattan chair from Java and local terrazzo flooring. *Above right:* Improvization at Villa Melati, Bali, transforms a tree bough into a clothes stand and a bamboo ladder into a towel rail.

Opposite: Accessories in Linda Garland's private bathroom all point to natural materials and indigenous manufacture. Woven bamboo walls become the perfect foil for shell-encrusted baskets, a mirror frame of shells, and a Javanese teapicker's basket recycled as a linen basket.

Above left: A circular skylight relieves oppression in this bathroom in a converted Singaporean shophouse. The steps accentuate the ceremonial aspect of bathing. *Above centre:* In this Singaporean bathroom, a traditional Chinese-style grille has been carved into the limestone wall and backed with a mirror. The generous steps can also function as shelves. *Above right:* Handwashing attains ritualistic dimensions at this island basin in a pool lined with black granite. Natural light comes from a skylight above, and the WC is hidden in a niche.

Opposite: Pebbles creep inside from an adjoining patio to surround simple wooden decking in a bathroom at Villa Melati, Bali. A chicken basket under the basin makes an original wastebin.

Sandrine Soimaud's house, also in Bali, you can take a stroll to admire the water plants of the walled garden and pluck a flower as you run your bath.

URBAN BATHROOMS

The absence of external space imposes a different attitude, one that architects of Singapore, Hong Kong and Bangkok strive to overcome with imagination. Chan Soo Khian of SCDA has managed to create what comes close to a bathroom with a spiritual edge by installing a brass, conical basin unit on a square slab surrounded by a pool of water and located directly beneath a skylight. That tiny step over the water adds a ritualistic quality to washing your hands. Similarly, a bathtub placed in an elevated position at the top of wide limestone steps imbues the bathing experience with a sense of ceremony, at the same time giving the bather a new visual perspective on the room and offering an easy dumping-ground for towels and bathrobes. In a more sombre mood, largely created by the slate-grey polished granite of the walls, HYLA Architects installed a jacuzzi tub on a raised platform, accessed by steps and separated by a glass partition from the rest of the bathroom. Again, the skylight alleviates what would otherwise be a claustrophobic space in a narrow, converted shophouse while simultaneously flooding the tub and its occupants with natural light.

Basketware

A nest of Malay wicker baskets offers instant receptacles for clothes, accessories, food or general household paraphernalia.

If there is one craft that is universal, it is basketware. Plants of all kinds have been used since time immemorial to weave containers, mats or roofs with varying levels of ingenuity and technique. Weave patterns and forms are as numerous as their functions, sometimes rendering the basic material virtually unrecognizable – as, for example, the painted Balinese baskets used to box wedding presents or Vietnam's upmarket coolie-hats that incorporate poems or embroidery. Throughout Asia, basketware is traditionally the women's work, learned from a young age and usually practised in communal fashion. Designed for and adapted to their particular function, the baskets may be worn on the back, stand on the floor, carry chickens, receive teapickers' leaves, sieve rice, trap fish or hold arrows. Imagination is not kept on hold, for contemporary forms continue to emerge, in particular from Bali and Kalimantan (Indonesia) and the Philippines.

Cross-border hilltribes such as the H'Mong of northern Thailand, Laos, Vietnam and southern China are adept at weaving rattan baskets for market produce. With their solid bases, the containers survive equally well strapped on the back or standing on the ground. They may not be as intricate as the fantastically embroidered cloths for which these minorities are known, but these sturdy market accessories are easily adaptable to a contemporary bathroom or bedroom, becoming useful despositories for towels or laundry. Less durable are the countless food baskets made from the flimsier pandanus palm. In Sabah, Borneo, strips of pandanus are dyed and then bound in vertical bands on a hat-shaped frame to create brilliantly coloured food-covers. Japan – not as well known for this craft as other Asian countries – produces basketware of woven split bamboo or maple, while the Chinese favour tiered wedding baskets of lacquered bamboo.

At the opposite end of the scale are baskets of such fine, intricate weaves that they resemble textiles. Rattan, easily available in Borneo's rainforests, is again the favoured plant for this purpose

as its strength and naturally shiny patina ensures a longer life than other materials. Borneo's formerly nomadic Punans excel in these complex creations, as do their neighbours the Iban. The striking geometric patterns in natural tones designed by the latter are now successfully transformed into non-traditional objects for export, such as wastepaper baskets, alongside the age-old and perennially popular floormat. In recent years plasticized raffia has been used in traditionally detailed weaves to create an idiosyncratic East–West fusion. Aceh, in northern Sumatra, has an equally long tradition of making sturdy, patterned rattan containers and boxes, while Bali specializes in *ata*, a local vine with impressive water-, heat- and insect-repelling qualities. This is now woven into a burgeoning range of bags, trays, boxes, bowls and placemats, often with black patterns. With increasing mass-production comes a simplification of technique, however, and many of the textural complexities are now being lost.

The prize for innovative basketware must go to the inhabitants of Kalimantan, where the decorative additions of cowrie shells to rims of large, wide baskets and woven boxes has become an industry in itself. In the Philippines *abaca* (native plant fibre) rushes and vines are woven to make shelving units and containers that suit contemporary Western-style interiors. On the other hand, an enduring basket form of South-East Asia is the rooster-basket; although its asymmetrical shape is designed to accommodate a crowing inmate, it adapts perfectly to numerous modern-day functions.

Above left: The simple cross-weave of Malay food baskets. *Above centre:* Complex *ata* baskets and containers are finely woven in eastern Bali from a local vine. *Above right:* Baskets and woven boxes edged with, or completely faced in, cowrie shells are a newly developed product of Indonesia, made in Kalimantan and marketed in Bali.

Resting

Given that a third of our lives is spent in repose, the space, atmosphere and comfort of the bedroom is of primordial importance. This is where we retreat to our inner worlds, eventually awaking to reconfront our lives. Having said that, the somatic need is such that sleep can be achieved under the most adverse conditions, and the bedroom per se is very much a development of comparatively recent, sophisticated societies. From the original northern Chinese *k'ang* (a raised heated platform also used for daytime activities such as sewing or preparing food) to Indian *charpoys* (beds of wood and rope), the *tatami* mat and the futon, today's Oriental bed style represents an East-West medley of canopy beds, day beds, elaborately carved headboards or Western mattresses laid in Zen style on wooden platforms. Perhaps the only common denominator lies in the soft, white swathes of the mosquito net, the ultimate symbol of the tropics.

TRADITIONAL BEDDING

In rural Asia many people still sleep communally, stretching out on mats in an area used a few hours previously for eating and socializing. In some cases woven bamboo or rush mats are so thin that it is akin to sleeping on floorboards, and there is not even a pillow for comfort. A major step up in style comes with Japanese *tatami* mats, a 500-year-old tradition that endures today. These woven bamboo mats, stuffed with rice-straw, edged with binding cloth and exuding a wonderful aroma of hay, are the classic portable bed. Accompanying them is a small, hard pillow designed for support rather than comfort. Greater comfort is provided by the cotton futon mattress, which can be folded in three or rolled up when not in use. During the day, when the same space is used for other activities, sleeping-mats, futons and quilts are stored in *oshi-ire* (built-in closets about 3 feet/90cm deep), which are closed with an opaque, sliding *fusama*.

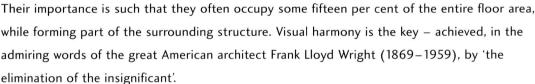

Their importance is such that they often occupy some fifteen per cent of the entire floor area, while forming part of the surrounding structure. Visual harmony is the key – achieved, in the admiring words of the great American architect Frank Lloyd Wright (1869–1959), by 'the elimination of the insignificant'.

In China, where the development of Oriental furniture began, the earliest beds excavated so far date from the 4th–3rd centuries BC. Astoundingly sophisticated, they consisted of black lacquered frames surrounded by low bamboo railings and held a sleeping base of bamboo, wood or matting. Six short carved legs supported the entire structure. Other beds from the same period held a sleeping base composed of three layers – bamboo strips, matting and silk wadding – and hinge mechanisms that enabled them to be folded away. During the Han dynasty (206 BC–AD 220), Emperor Ling demonstrated a marked penchant for chairs and beds imported from Tibet and Turkestan, and by the 6th century furniture – including canopy beds – had become established. With the movement of monks and traders, these forms spread throughout Asia and left a visible influence, even in Japan.

Take a vast leap in time to 1620 and you find a Chinese scholar, Wen Zhenheng, passing comment on the plethora of Ming dynasty bed designs. 'The small lacquered Song and Yuan dynasty beds are the best, the next being the single beds in palace style and after that the small

Above left: Intricate woodcarving salvaged from a Burmese temple frames a bed in Ou Baholyodhin's guest apartment; its workmanship is echoed by a silver incense-burner. *Above centre:* A copy of a Chinese clothes-stand in Nagara's Bangkok bedroom. *Above right:* A sober composition of colour and line.

Opposite: Amnad Khitipanna's Bangkok bedroom is separated from a study area by an ornate screen made with beams from a northern Thai temple and a panel from a 19th-century Chinese bridal bed. A lacquered Thai barrel acts as a bedside table.

Previous page: Versatility is the key to the main pavilion at Villa Tirta Ayu, Bali. The foreground area acts as living space or guest bedroom and can be separated from the master bedroom beyond by the sliding, screenprinted canvas doors.

Reinterpretations of the Western curtain tie-back make effective use of local materials. *Above left:* Complex threaded shellwork designed by Linda Garland. *Above right:* Coarse hessian rope twisted through a wooden ring.

Opposite: The lengths of white muslin draped around this handcarved bed at the Tugu Hotel, Bali, provide privacy while allowing ambient light to penetrate.

wooden pieces made by fine craftsmen. If the bamboo beds, canopied beds and beds with antechambers are polychrome lacquer or bear geometric designs, they are *su* … ' The dreaded, condemnatory word *su* (vulgar) was the opposite of the target style, *ya* (refined), and equivalent to the Western concept of kitsch – definitely to be avoided.

CANOPY BEDS

Four- or six-poster beds, veritable rooms within rooms, comprised detachable posts and railings topped with a canopy of decorative panels or fabric. This form is still popular in grand residences of Bali, where the four posters may even be incorporated into the beam structure of the pavilion. Another variation, found at Bali's Tugu hotel, is the tent-like canopy created by stretching fabric over a wooden armature to give an exhilirating sense of height. Javanese canopy beds, which were the inspiration for the Balinese model, are composed of carved openwork panels surrounding three sides of the bed, often with a carved lintel in front. Draped with textiles or net, they produce a soporific sense of enclosure and security. Pictures or beautiful textiles can be hung inside to increase the suggestion of a separate, personal space.

As increasingly elaborate canopied beds became the norm in wealthy households of China, so the separate bedroom developed to accommodate their immovable bulkiness. However, the

curtained haven of the bed itself meant that the bedroom could also serve other functions, such as washing, calligraphy or even receiving guests. Beautifully carved Ming washstands of *huanghuali* wood were commonplace in the bedroom, Chinese culture making less of a ritual of the washing activity than the Japanese. Equally visible were carved clothes stands, ideal for suspending the voluminous robes of the time, as well as camphorwood chests for clothes storage and tables for taking tea. During the day, the lavish hangings around the bed would be hooked back to enable the bed to function as a sofa.

Canopy beds are rare in Thailand, but the wooden structure is more intricate in form. Curved Chinese legs often support lavishly carved, semi-enclosed bed frames and majestic headboards, so that the bed is a major focal point in the room. Thai and Burmese carved dressing tables are equally opulent in style, low for kneeling at and with large fitted mirrors.

DAY BEDS

In the same fluid way, beds found their way into other parts of a Chinese house. The gentleman's domain of the study traditionally contained a day bed or couch for the master to recover from his arduous mental activity. The couch bed (a development of the *k'ang*), with three sides enclosed by a low, openwork railing or carved panels, later became known as the

Above left: Brilliant silks are juxtaposed in these cushions by Princess & Thepea, piled on a 19th-century Chinese day bed at Lajeunesse Gallery, Singapore. *Above right:* This precious early 20th-century ceremonial silk *lampung* from Cambodia is woven with gold thread on both sides to make a heavy brocade.

Opposite: A living space at the Begawan Giri's Uma Bona royal suite is dominated by a centrally placed day bed composed of Thai silk cushions. The glass-fronted cabinets from Palembang, Sumatra, lacquerware from Myanmar and brassware from Java all contribute to a sense of richness and decorative detail.

opium bed for obvious reasons. The base of wood, matting or rattan, together with its form, strongly echoed the prehistoric versions mentioned above. With the mushrooming of opium smoking during the 18th–19th centuries, these beds became increasingly ornate, in tune with Qing dynasty tastes. Numerous blackwood versions inlaid with mother-of-pearl and marble panels still exist in the overseas Chinese communities of Singapore, Malaysia and Vietnam. Screens were often placed around day beds to simulate an enclosed space, so creating an impermanent room within a room.

An indiosyncratic version of the day bed can be found in some contemporary Thai homes: finely carved couches with repeated ripples of inwardly curving legs are in fact reworked from elephant howdahs (seats). Piled high with cushions of Thai silk, they make inviting daytime reclining areas. Another use of the Chinese *ta*, or day bed, is made by Nagara, in Bangkok. As his fashion-designer status demands extensive clothes storage, he has created a separate dressing room. The entire central space of the room is occupied by a large wooden day bed in classical Chinese style; perfect for laying clothes on, the bed also doubles as a table. Similarly, at the Begawan Giri in Bali, the centre of a living area in a suite is taken up by a vast day bed with triangular Thai cushions backing both ends. This becomes a communal lounging area, where tea can be served, cards played, books devoured or siestas induced – all in consummate splendour.

Above left: A cinnabar-red Chinese cupboard harmonizes with a Klungklung ikat, a Balinese bowl and lacquered pots from Sumatra and China. *Above centre:* A reclining elephant god, Ganesha, inspires sleep in Bill Bensley's master bedroom in Bangkok. An antique Burmese medicine chest becomes a functional headboard, while the bold geometry of the masks matches that of the cushions. *Above right:* From a veranda at the Puri Merta, Bali, gilded openwork screens frame a view into a bedroom and to the outdoor bathroom beyond, giving an overall impression of lightness and space.

Opposite: Seen through a shuttered window, this bedrom at Villa Sawah, Bali, offers daytime repose on a day bed from Madura and nocturnal sleep in a massive Javanese bed. All the structural woodwork is limewashed to enhance the sense of light.

In both cases, we witness the Oriental habit of concentrating furniture in the centre of a room rather than at its edges, as in the West.

Contemporary Asian alternatives to heavy wood used for beds are indigenous materials such as bamboo (exemplified by Linda Garland's designs in Bali), rattan or wicker, all of which provide a cool, lightweight bed structure that can easily be moved around. These are produced mainly for export in Indonesia and the Philippines.

STORAGE SYSTEMS

Clothes storage, that universal headache, has long been catered for in the East by extensive use of chests (aromatic, insect-repelling camphorwood is particularly popular with the Chinese), trunks and cabinets. The now ubiquitous cinnabar-red lacquered cupboard in classical Ming style is just one of many forms that have evolved. All stand on short legs and most have removable interior shelves – again, allowing for change. Brass or pewter locks, plates and hinges often become decorative features in themselves, although traditionally the doors pivoted on dowels to preserve the clean lines of the design. When each cupboard door is composed of two sections, the upper part may be of geometric, openwork carving. Chinese cupboard shelving was always symmetrically arranged, unlike Japanese shelving, which is invariably asymmetrical. This same Chinese sense of balance is seen in the making of cupboards and side tables in pairs. In Thailand, carved and/or painted cabinets often follow the form of house structures – lines sloping gently outwards towards the base, which, like the Chinese model, is raised on carved legs or, occasionally, a plinth.

Chests may be of lacquered wood, of fine bamboo strips or of bark studded with cowrie shells, while Chinese camphorwood trunks are generally covered in lacquered vellum or pigskin, both of which take on a patina with the years. Both Korea and Japan developed their own forms from the Chinese model. The Korean chest was highly elaborate in terms of hinges and lock plates, while the Japanese version ranged from a decorated form with lacquered landscapes to the sturdy but portable *tansu*. Although the Japanese used built-in wardrobes to store sleeping materials, they always stored their most precious items in the *tansu*, tangible evidence of a justifiable fear of fire in their wood and paper houses. Designed to be airtight so as to preserve fragile documents and fabrics, and lined with cedarwood or lead, the *tansu* is fitted with carrying handles and even retractable wheels. It is not for nothing that the traditional Japanese woman's dress, the kimono, is cut on a rectangular pattern that makes it easy to fold away and stack vertically. Portability, and thus impermanence, are never far away in the Oriental spirit.

Above: A theme of red and gold, the Balinese predilection, is repeated in headboard, cushions and canopy in a faithful copy of the bedroom of the artist Le Mayeur at the Tugu Hotel, Bali.

Opposite: Faded splendour rules in this sleeping pavilion at the Puri Anyar in Bali. The bed structure, integrated into the beams, is crowned by a mythical Balinese lion, the symbol of power. A shrine for offerings is attached to a bedpost.

Textiles

Textiles in their multifarious weaves, colours, designs and materials lend immediate softness and originality to an interior. Asia offers an almost boundless choice, from the subtle, cotton ikats and batiks of Indonesia to sumptuous Chinese or Vietnamese embroidered silks and satins, diaphanous Indian muslins and the intricate embroideries and weavings of the hilltribes of Indo-China and Thailand. In between these generalized points are endless regional variations, including the vivid cottons of Orissa, India, the strong geometric designs of Lombok, Indonesia, subtle *pua* (warp ikats) of Borneo, ceremonial embroidered tapis of Sumatra and the numerous incarnations of Thai silk. No other region in the world is home to such an extraordinary range, a factor that contributed greatly to Asia's internal trade as well as to its early links with the West.

Chinese silk, a six-thousand-year-old craft, set the Silk Road into motion and gave the ancient Greeks and Romans their word for silk, *serica*, which also means people who wear silk robes or, by extension, the Chinese. Weaving and embroidery blossomed under the Tang dynasty, at which time the bazaars of the Middle East brimmed with imported Chinese cloths. Today's silk products often emanate from Vietnam, where sericulture was developed under Chinese rule during the first millennium AD. However, the fragile nature of embroidered silk, ill-adapted to tropical humidity, makes it suitable only for framed display. More robust is the lustrous *songket* (silk brocade) still handwoven in parts of Malaysia and Indonesia. The technique, which incorporates gold or silver threads, came with Islam.

Cotton ikat (which means 'tie' or 'bind' in Malay) is perhaps the most easily adaptable textile for contemporary interiors because of its dense, earthy colours, bold geometric designs and heavy, durable cloth. Authentic handspun, handwoven ikats made with vegetable dyes are, however, increasingly hard to find, and their prices are rising in consequence. The original technique is

Silk *songket* (brocade) from the Malay peninsula, one of Asia's richest fabrics, is generally reserved for weddings.

 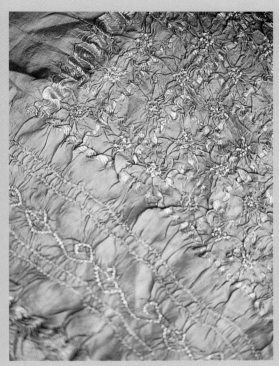 

complex, involving binding warp threads on a loom with dye-resistant fibres in order to create a predetermined design before plunging them into dye vats. Successive binding and dyeing of threads builds up the overall pattern. The fabric is then woven with either plain or similarly tie-dyed wefts (the latter creating the rare double-ikat cloth of Bali).

Ikat motifs such as spirals, diamonds, hooks and meanders are thought to have been inspired by the prehistoric Dong Son culture of Vietnam, brought to Indonesia in the form of bronze drums. Others originated in Chinese and Indian cultures, while lizards, crocodiles, birds and geckos are common animist symbols. Quality ikat textiles have deep spiritual and ceremonial functions, with specific colours and designs that are associated with life-cycle events such as birth, death or marriage.

India's fount of glorious textiles has been pillaged by neighbours since prehistoric times for its inventiveness, dazzling colours and embroidered or appliqué additions. In the 15th century, Java, Sumatra and Bali started importing double-ikat *patola* silk (with geometric designs) from Gujarat, and antique examples are now collectors' items. Both Rajasthan and Gujarat have long been sources of strikingly colourful embroidered cottons that would serve as anything from bullock covers to shawls, door or wall hangings and even ceiling awnings. Equally prolific and inventive are today's textile centres of Orissa and Andhra Pradesh, while the luscious silks of Varanasi and Kanchipuram, in southern India, are generally destined for use as clothing rather than in the home.

Above left: The intricate technique employed to create this Thai hilltribe embroidery is shared by minority peoples in Vietnam, Laos and China. *Above centre:* The ruched effect and shirring of Gujarati tie-dye silk is enhanced by gold thread and discreet use of paint. *Above right:* Silk and cotton are mixed in these embroidered panels from western China.

Surrounding Space

Landscape views, communicating pavilions, walkways, formal gardens, courtyards and contemplative pools are all essential elements of the space surrounding Asian homes. In the tropical belt that this book concentrates on, the exterior becomes an integral part of the interior, whereby lines, colours, sounds and even fragrances are projected inside. Traditional Western boundaries between inside and outside disappear and, in the open-sided pavilions of Bali, Java, Cambodia and Thailand, a room may be nothing more than a roofed space without walls. The exterior is also brought inside in more subtle ways: the shadow of a branch thrown onto a translucent Japanese screen contrasts its oblique curve with the formality of the geometrical interior; an emerald-green padi-field view becomes a living picture when framed by a carved Javanese windowframe; a thickly forested slope seen through the glazed walls of a contemporary Balinese house imparts the sensation of living in the treetops.

In contrast to the closed and compartmentalized homes of the West, the openness inherent in Asian houses generates changing perspectives and visual communication. Verandas and inner courtyards merge the opposites of inside and out, while spatial distinctions become obliterated by sliding walls, the archetypal symbol of versatile living. Doors are noticeable by their absence and, if present, are not to keep heat in, as in the West, but to act as security devices, albeit in imaginative and highly decorative forms. In this openness of structure, perspectives flow in many directions, bringing an awareness of space, of infinite potential and of transience. The sensation of being 'boxed in' is unknown.

THE VERANDA

Encapsulating the very notion of inside–outside living is the veranda, that transitional space and shadowy haven that epitomizes the tropics. Temperatures that are constant year round, combined

with periods of heavy rain and intense sunlight, mean that this roofed but wall-less space becomes the ideal multi-functional retreat and a viable alternative to indoor living. In traditional societies, the veranda is used for drying grains, making handicrafts or entertaining guests, while in more sophisticated houses it becomes a seamless extension of the interior. The habit is deeply rooted: nearly every Indonesian hotel room, however modest, has a private, roofed 'sit-out' furnished with armchairs and a table where afternoon tea is served – the perfect setting for taking stock of the day or for watching the rhythm of the rains. More evolved domestic versions accommodate day beds and wicker or rattan furniture, the ongoing products of Filipino and Indonesian designers. Even in Singapore, where space is precious, neo-modernist houses on limited plots manage to incorporate that same transitional area. With the property protected by an outer wall and maybe by a shield of vegetation, security and privacy are assured.

Elaborately carved fretwork edging the eaves in the Malay-style veranda adds definition to external views, while balustrades, potted plants and natural vegetation create a notion of separation where the deck ends. A contemporary, offbeat alternative on a Bangkok veranda is a motley array of suspended birdcages culled from the local fleamarket, all empty and all painted in white. This decorative arrangement successfully corrupts the Asian hobby of caging songbirds while screening the view of distant highrises. Pillars supporting the roof can be of smooth, natural wood or carved

Left: Fretwork balustrades and arches add graphic character to this veranda at the Tugu Hotel in Bali. The lines of the Javanese sofa reflect Indonesia's colonial Dutch influences.

Opposite: The Bangkok veranda of landscape designer Bill Bensley is screened by a mass of tropical vegetation, while creepers snake downwards from a trellis roof. The chair is from northern Thailand and the storage jar from China.

Previous page: Water, vegetation and light surround the living wing of Mrs Leonora Tan's Singapore house, an extreme contemporary application of Asia's traditional affinities. Blinds of weatherproofed canvas act as shields against the rain, but otherwise this is is pared-down living attuned to the tropics.

Above left: A Pakistani *jali* screen inserted into a balcony wall at Bill Bensley's house in Bangkok facilitates lateral ventilation. The cement bench is faced in tiles and a trunk serves as a coffee table. *Above centre:* Fronting the master bedroom in Sandrine Soimaud's Balinese house is a deep veranda, its overhang shading the glazed walls from the sun. Suspended glass shelves display a collection of Majapahit-style terracotta figures, while a primitive Javanese hornbill sculpture stands below. *Above right:* The veranda roof at Carole Muller's house in Bali is supported by slender pillars set into bases of cast cement or carved in volcanic stone.

Opposite: A flowing perspective at the Puri Merta, Bali, leads the eye from a bedroom through a veranda to a raised *bale* (pavilion), where meals are taken.

and/or painted in elaborate Thai style. The sloping overhang itself is thatched or tiled on top, while the underside is either clad with woven bamboo matting or timber, or is simply left with tile-pattern and rafters revealed.

In Japan, coarse linen banners sometimes separate outer and inner space. Elsewhere, where protection from the sun's rays is necessary at certain times of day, billowing white cotton curtains (inappropriate in humid conditions) soften the structure and lend a glowing opacity. Reed or bamboo blinds filter the light in a more structured way, allowing variations in shade and view and also functioning effectively as a shield against winds and driving rain. Any one of these methods radically and instantly transforms the feel of the space and, once again, emphasizes its inherent flexibility.

COURTYARDS AND WALKWAYS

Defining the perimeter of Asian homes are stone or brick walls or bamboo fencing. The most ornate gateways are those of Bali, traditionally split and having a freestanding inner wall that fulfills the same purpose as the Chinese spirit wall in deflecting malevolent spirits and leaving the entrance open to circulation yet visually contained.

As these enclosure walls often harbour multi-generational or multi-family clusters in separate pavilions, the shared common ground is the courtyard, an essential stage-set for social interaction.

The ultimate model of the courtyard house is the northern Chinese *siheyuan*, in which single-storey buildings around the outer compound walls overlook an ordered central space, sometimes subdivided further according to social hierarchy. Seniority is also acknowledged, with older members of the family located at the back, sons and their families at the sides, and more active parts of the household (servants' quarters, kitchen, storage) in the front. A narrow walkway-cum-veranda is created by the projected eaves of these buildings, while the courtyard itself houses symmetrically planted trees and paved paths.

For urban societies where space is at a premium, the Chinese shophouse has become an enduring model, famously revitalized by the architect Tadao Ando in Osaka in the 1970s. Built on a deep, narrow plot, the shophouse incorporates an internal courtyard or lightwell, which in some contemporary conversions of Singapore is transformed into a pool for contemplative, aesthetic and cooling purposes.

Many rural Japanese houses, too, are based on this concept – but with a twist. Shintoism's emphasis on nature transforms the internal courtyard into a garden punctuated by stepping-stones, boulders and stone lanterns. The importance of this area is such that years may be spent shifting the stones before the required visual balance is achieved. In Sri Lanka, the patio tradition, which originated in Roman times, and was imported by Arab and later Portuguese traders and settlers, has

Above left: A cool, intimate courtyard at the Tugu Hotel, Bali, is created by an overhead trellis, in turn softened by flowering creepers. The carved and painted doors were salvaged from a local house. *Above centre:* Bill Bensley created these exterior lamps in his Bangkok garden by joining bell-shaped bamboo cock-cages and covering them in cotton. *Above right:* A shrine, inset Chinese plates and a carved gateway mark the entrance to a courtyard at the Puri Merta, Bali.

Opposite: Restful symmetry: this landmark design by Geoffrey Bawa, in Colombo, Sri Lanka, epitomizes inside–outside living perfectly. The form of a rectangular pool is reflected in an overhead opening between pitched, tiled eaves that direct the flow of the monsoon rain. Natural materials are used throughout.

Different styles of walkway. *Above left:* Nagara's uncovered, tiled-floor version in Bangkok, which zigzags across a water garden. *Above centre:* Sandrine Soimaud's irregular Balinese walkway, its overhang supported by coconut-palm trunks and with decking made of recycled container planks. *Above right:* Mr and Mrs John Tan's L-shaped walkway in Singapore, with its tiled overhang, parallel water channel and louvred screens that filter the light.

been revived and multiplied by the architect Geoffrey Bawa. As a result, his houses may offer a series of perspectives from inner to outer to inner, alternating light with shade, allowing easy air circulation and bringing glimpses of vegetation or water into the heart of the house.

In the tropics, covered walkways are essential during periods of intense sun or rainfall in order to move painlessly from one part of the house to another. Some innovative Chinese variations resulted from 4th-century social rivalry when a certain Wang K'ai ordered a superior silk-shaded walkway of 40 *li* (20km, or 12 miles). His neighbour, Shih Ch'ung, subsequently built one that was bigger and better: measuring 50 *li*, it was protected by silk brocade. As silk canopies are not the most recommended outdoor material, today's walkways are either thatched or tiled. They can be separate entities from the house or, more commonly, as found in northern China and in Geoffrey Bawa's Sri Lankan houses, are created by giving the roof a deep, colonnaded overhang.

A contemporary application of this is found at Sandrine Soimaud's house in Bali, built according to an irregular, elongated plan. Rooms are connected on one façade by a series of verandas and on the other by a roofed walkway of wooden decking that follows the structural contours. Here, judiciously placed furniture – a cupboard, a chair and table – dispels any notion of distance or monotony, and the garden becomes an integral visual element of the open-sided circuit. In the case of Nagara's home in Bangkok, simple tiled walkways edged by metal balustrades become bridges as

they crisscross the luxuriant vegetation of the water garden, giving the sensation of penetrating a strangely ordered tropical forest as one moves from one pavilion to the next.

WATER, WATER EVERYWHERE

More than anything else, it is the presence of water that characterizes the immediate surroundings of an Asian house. Reflective, contemplative, purifying, soothing, cooling, water is the ultimate accompaniment for outdoor living. More pragmatically, an estimated fifty-four per cent of the world's population lives on the Asian waterfront of coastlines, canals and riverbanks. Not least, the hybrid culture of the entire region owes much to the cross-pollinating instincts of early seafarers (see pages 14–16).

Buddhism again intervenes. It was the symbolism of Mount Meru's cosmic ocean that required temples and monasteries to be located beside water, whether river, moat, lake or lotus pond, while Buddha's enlightenment took place in front of a river. Some temples were built so close to the water's edge that from certain angles they appear to rise out of the depths: the two halves of a whole, the building and its reflection, yin and yang. This is exemplified by Kyoto's Gold Temple (Kinkakuji), originally built as a summer house, by Cambodia's Angkor Wat and by Bali's towering *meru* (pagoda) at Lake Bratan (see photographs on pages 14 and 15).

Sliding and removable glazed walls and a lotus pond characterize this contemporary interpretation of a Balinese pavilion in Sydney, Australia, by architect Peter Stutchbury for the jewellery designer Wendy Parker.

In the domestic sphere, this approach is taken to its extreme in Wong Mun Summ's design of Mrs Leonora Tan's house in Singapore. By projecting the two wings of the house into water, the standard tropical garden is replaced by a huge pool, its transparent depths faced by brilliant turquoise tiles reminiscent of a painting by David Hockney (1937–). When hunger strikes, you can swim from the living wing to the dining wing, though luckily there are also land routes on two sides. Equally total in coverage, but enclosed within the structure of a two-storeyed suite, is a private pool at the Begawan Giri hotel in Bali. This ingenious design by Cheong Yew Kuan offers visual perspectives from the upper floor of an internal watery expanse open to the skies. On the lower floor you can shower in the bathroom before taking the plunge through large openings at water level. Similarly, though the spatial coverage of water is not so great, John Tan's Singapore house is constructed around carp ponds. Flashes of fish among the water lilies are thus visible from the kitchen, the living room and the two-storey bridge that connects the two sections of the house. As carp and water are both Chinese symbols of luck and prosperity, this house would seem destined to flourish.

Carp also enter the landscape of Carole Muller's Balinese house, where water is exploited as a pure sensual treat. As the building overlooks the water palace of Tirtagangga, vast pools of fresh spring water fill the middle distance before the horizon ends at the sea. In the immediate

Above left: The Chinese perceive carp as symbols of good luck and, whenever possible, bring them close to the home, a habit that has been adopted in Singapore. *Above right:* The visual purity of the infinity-edge pool at Sandrine Soimaud's house in Bali is punctuated by two *bale* (open-sided pavilions).

Opposite: The ever-changing, stress-relieving qualities of water are an integral part of Asian design. Here, at the Tugu Hotel, Bali, a large pond reflects tropical vegetation and the coastal skies.

137

Above left: Varying textures of pebble and stone add contrast to the internal pools at this Singaporean house. *Above right:* A dramatic stepped pool faced in green-, grey- and sand-coloured tiles creates a mirror to the elements at the Begawan Giri, Bali.

Opposite, left: A balustraded walkway at Mr and Mrs John Tan's house in Singapore looks out over the lily-pond towards the folding doors of the living room. *Opposite, right:* Allying history, sumptuousness and modernity, this internal pool at a suite of the Begawan Giri, Bali, is accessible from lower-floor bathrooms or down steps from above. The majestic focal point is a 14th-century Majapahit stupa.

surroundings of this elevated house, a series of lotus ponds offers aesthetic nourishment for guests in the open *bale* (pavilion), and luxuriant flowering shrubs are echoed in pots of bonsai frangipani trees placed along the veranda wall. *'Luxe, calme et volupté'* rules. In a similar vein, Amnad Khitipanna's house on the fringes of Bangkok employs a long perspective over a meandering lake to lead the eye through a Japanese-style bridge to a focal-point folly at the end.

The universal appeal of swimming pools has produced imaginative versions that eschew incongruity or mere functionality in order to blend into their surroundings. A common feature of Far Eastern landscapes are water-filled padi-fields, their shimmering surfaces acquiring an almost metallic quality towards dusk. At Sandrine Soimaud's house, this image is re-created in a freeform pool whose razor-sharp profile merges with a backdrop of terraced padi-fields just a few metres beyond. In another nod to local forms, raised, open-sided pavilions at each end of the pool offer lounging areas for swimmers, and their projecting decks double as diving boards. Also in Bali, the architect Martin Smyth decided to test the mettle of anyone using the pool at Villa Melati by perching it on the very edge of the Ayung gorge. Swim to the curved outer rim and you look straight down a vertiginous drop to rushing torrents a couple of hundred metres below. Seen from the house, this pool, lined with mottled green mosaic, acts as a mirror to the forested hillside behind and the shifting cloudscapes above. Once again, the outside moves in and opposites meet.

Directory

ARCHITECTS & DESIGNERS

Ou Baholyodhin 12 Greatorex St, London E1 5NF, UK.
Email: oub@globalnet.co.uk

Bill Bensley Bensley Design Studios, 167/1 Soi Ekamai 5,
Sukhumvit Rd 63, Bangkok 10110, Thailand.
Email: bensley@mozart.inet.co.th

Cheong Yew Kuan AREA, 49 Cantonment Rd,
Singapore 089748. Email: area@indo.net.id

Linda Garland *See Hotels and Accommodation below.*

HYLA Architects 47 Ann Siang Rd, 02-01, Singapore
06970. Email: info@hyla.co.sg

William Lim 179 River Valley Rd, Singapore 179033.
Email: wlap@pacific.net.sg

SCDA 10 Teck Lim Rd, Singapore 088386.
Email: scda@cyberway.co.sg

WOHA Designs 136 Bukit Timah Rd, Singapore 229838.
Email: woha@cyberway.com.sg

HOTELS AND ACCOMMODATION IN THE ASIAN STYLE

* Asterisked establishments are featured in this book.

Ana Mandara Tran Phu Blvd, Nha Trang, Vietnam
Tel: + 84 (0)58 829829 Fax: +84 (0)58 829629
Email: eamamr@dng.vnn.vn *A pavilion-style, beachside hotel
with marked Vietnamese design features.*

Bali Tropical Villas Seminyak, Bali, Indonesia. Tel/fax: + 62
(0)361 732083 www.bali-tropical-villas.com *A wide choice
of European-owned villas in Bali for rent.*

Bali Villas PO Box 1090, Tubun, Bali, Indonesia.
Tel: + 62 (0)361 703060 Fax: + 62 (0)361 701577
www.balivillas.com *A wide selection of private villas available
to rent in Bali.*

Begawan Giri* Dusun Melingghih Kelod, Ubud, Bali 80571,
Indonesia. Tel: + 62 (0)361 978888, UK reservations tel:
0800 169 8817 Fax: + 62 (0)361 978889
Email: begawan@indo.net.id www.designhotels.com *Set in
padi-style bliss outside Ubud, this pavilion retreat is touted as
one of the world's most luxurious and innovative hotels. Interior
styles vary from tribal to Japanese, Javanese and Imperial
Chinese. Designed by Cheong Yew Kuan.*

The Chedi Ubud* Desa Melinggih Kelod, Payangan, Bali
85072, Indonesia. Tel: + 62 (0)361 975963,
UK reservations tel: 0800 169 8817 Fax: + 62 (0)361
975968 www.designhotels.com *Interesting Asian details*

integrated into a contemporary hotel.

The Datai Jalan Teluk Datai, 07000 Pulau Langkawi,
Malaysia. Tel: + 60 (0)4 959 2500 Fax: + 60 (0)4 959
2600 Email: datai@ghmhotels.com *Designed by Wong Mun
Summ of WOHA Designs, a beautifully crafted tropical forest
hotel revelling in the finest Asian materials.*

Duxton Hotel 83 Duxton Rd, Singapore 089540.
Tel: + 65 (0)227 7678 Fax: + 65 (0)227 1232
Email: duxton@singnet.com.sg www.duxtonhotels.com.sg
*Intriguingly converted Chinese shophouses, high on antiques, in
the heart of Chinatown.*

Linda Garland Estate* PO Box 196, Ubud, 80571 Bali,
Indonesia. Tel: + 62 (0)361 974028 Fax: + 62 (0)361
974029 www.lindagarland.com *A large, undulating property
at Nyuh Kuning. Bamboo houses for rent, designed and furnished
by Linda Garland. State-of-the-art outdoor bathrooms.*

Pangkor Laut Resort Pulau Pangkor, 32200 Lumut,
Malaysia. Tel: + 60 (0)5 699 1100 Fax: + 60 (0)5 699
1200 Email: plr@po.jaring.my *Pavilion-style architecture on
stilts in the Strait of Malacca. Designed by Lek Bunnag and Bill
Bensley with Thai, Malay and Indonesian accents.*

Puri Merta* Jalan Pengubungan Banjar Silayukti, Kerobokan,
Bali, Indonesia www.soneva-pavilion.com *A delightful
evocation of Balinese pavilion style, with changing levels and lush
vegetation, by Australian designer Made Wijaya.*

The Regent Resort Mae Rim, Chiang Mai, Thailand.
Email: rcm.reservations@fourseasons.com *Lanna-style
architecture and northern Thai crafts in the lap of luxury.*

Tugu Hotel Bali* Canggu Beach, Bali, Indonesia.
Email: bali@tuguhotels.com *Dubbed the 'museum hotel' for
its fabulous amalgamation of Javanese and Balinese antiques
with local architectural features.*

MUSEUMS

Agung Rai Museum of Art Ubud, Bali, Tel: + 62 (0)361
976659 Email: armaubud@denpasar.wasantara.net.id
www.chica.com/arma *Performing arts centre and collection of
Balinese artforms in impressively scaled traditional buildings.*

Asian Civilisations Museum 39 Armenian St, Singapore
179941. Tel: + 65 (0)332 3573 *A rare display of the
Peranakan (Straits Chinese) legacy showing its 19th-century
mastery of inlay, textiles, silverwork, porcelain and furniture.*

Percival David Foundation 53 Gordon Square, London
WC1H OPD, UK. Tel: + 44 (0)20 7387 3909 *Quite
simply the finest collection of Chinese ceramics outside China.*

Suan Pakkad Palace Museum 352–354 Sri Ayudhya Rd,
Rajathevi, Bangkok 10400, Thailand. Tel: + 66 (0)2 246
1775/6 Fax: + 66 (0)2 247 2079 *Six traditional

reconstructed Thai houses with stunning 17th–18th-century
lacquered pavilion, furniture and antiques.*

Jim Thompson House and Museum 6 Soi Kasemsan 2,
Rama 1 Rd, Bangkok, Thailand. Tel: + 66 (0)2 216 7368
Fax: + 66 (0)2 612 3744 *The quintessential example of a
transplanted Westerner's passion for his adopted culture,
housed in a traditional klong (canal) house.*

SHOPS AND SUPPLIERS

AUSTRALIA

Au Lion des Neiges 76 Queen St, Woollahra, NSW 2022.
Tel: + 61 (0)2 9362 0115 *Antiques from Tibet, Nepal,
Bhutan and Mongolia.*

Bali in Profile 81 Pacific Highway, Roseville, NSW 206.
Tel: + 61 (0)2 9413 1622 *Indonesian furniture, decorative
pieces, stoneware and assorted artefacts.*

Cheeky Tiger Shop 9, Central Ave, Manly, NSW 2095.
Tel: + 61 (0)2 9976 6133 *Oriental furniture, fabrics,
ceramics and assorted artefacts.*

Chinese Antique Company 160 Oxford St, Woollahra,
NSW 2025. Tel: + 61 (0)2 9327 8840 *Chinese and
Japanese furniture, porcelain and assorted artefacts.*

Chosan Oriental Gallery 993 Pacific Highway, Pymble,
NSW 2073. Tel: + 61 (0)2 9488 9298 *Korean and
Japanese furniture and art objects.*

Ergo Lifestyle Stores Shop 116A, Warringah Mall, Pittwater
Rd, Brookvale, NSW 2100. Tel: + 61 (0)2 9938 4799
Chinese furniture and porcelain.

Kazari 290 Malvern Rd, Prahran, VIC 3181. Tel: + 61 (0)3
9521 1107 *Japanese and Chinese furniture and
decorative objects.*

Made in Japan 437 Oxford St, Paddington, NSW 2021.
Tel: + 61 (0)2 9360 6979; 28 Victor St, Chatswood, NSW
2067. Tel: + 61 (0)2 9410 3799 *Japanese furnishings.*

Soo Tze Oriental Antiques 46 Commercial Rd, Prahran,
VIC 3181. Tel: + 61 (0)3 9521 2892 *Antiques and textiles.*

HONG KONG

Chinese Arts and Crafts Centre Tsim Cha Tsui St, Central,
Hong Kong. Tel: + 852 2839 1888. *Chinese furnishings and
decorative objects.*

INDONESIA

Shalimar Ubud main street, Ubud, Bali.
Email: shalimar@idola.net.id *Large selection of antique textiles
from all over South-East Asia.*

Tegun Jalan Hanuman 44, Ubud, Bali. Tel/fax: + 62 (0)361
973361 *Good selection of Balinese crafts, including ikat.*

NEW ZEALAND

Buana Satu 229 Karangahape Road, Auckland Central, Auckland. Tel: + 64 (0)9 358 5561 *Indonesian furniture, homewares, artefacts and mats.*

Corso De' Fiori 8 George Street, Parnell, Auckland. Tel: + 64 (0)9 307 9166; corner of Aikmans & Papanui Roads, Merivale, Christchurch. Tel: + 64 (0)3 355 4228 *Chinese antique furniture, decor items, linen and porcelain; furniture from the Philippines; Thai pots and pewterware.*

Higashi 31 Kingdon Street, Newmarket, Auckland. Tel: + 64 (0)9 520 7107; Level 3, Atrium on Elliott, Elliott Street, Auckland City. Tel: + 64 (0)9 379 8188 www.higashi.co.nz *Japanese crockery, homewares, textiles, boxes, antique furniture.*

Margaret Muir Design Unit G, 132 Marua Road, Ellerslie, Auckland. Tel: + 64 (0)9 525 3000 *Restored antique Chinese furniture, Asian-influenced contemporary furniture made from recycled Chinese timber, and embroidered bedlinen.*

Obelisk 161 Victoria Street, Christchurch. Tel: + 64 (0)3 365 1500 www.obelisk.co.nz *Indian furniture, baskets, textiles, soft furnishings and decor items.*

Redcurrent 63 Ponsonby Road, Ponsonby, Auckland. Tel: + 64 (0)9 361 1003; 143 Victoria Street, Christchurch. Tel: + 64 (0)3 365 8040 *Thai bamboo furniture and homewares; Chinese lacquered furniture, trunks and porcelain; Indonesian furniture; seagrass baskets from the Philippines; Vietnamese lacquerware.*

The Third Eye 117 Karangahape Road, Auckland Central. Tel: + 64 (0)9 379 8739 *Indian furniture, soft furnishings and artefacts; Nepali and Tibetan decorative items.*

Wade House 202 Hutt Road, Kaiwharawhara, Wellington. Tel: + 64 (0)4 499 8885 *Chinese antique furniture and decorative items.*

World House 55 The Strand, Parnell, Auckland. Tel: + 64 (0)9 303 2070 *Furniture from central Java.*

Zenophile 87 Jervois Road, Herne Bay, Auckland. Tel: + 64 (0)9 360 8984 *Japanese crystal, ceramics, cast-iron teapots, floor-cushions and lighting; Vietnamese lacquerware, lighting, furniture and homewares; Tibetan carpets.*

SINGAPORE

Lajeunesse Asian Art 94 Club St, Singapore 069462. Email: lajeune@lajeunesseasianart.com *Asian artefacts, objets d'art and textiles, particularly from China and Myanmar.*

Loong Art Gallery 262/262A South Bridge Rd, Singapore 058811. Email: loongart@pacific.net.sg *Antique Chinese furniture, trunks and ancestor paintings.*

Pagoda House Gallery 44 & 49 Pagoda St,

Singapore 059208. Tel/fax: + 65 (0)225 8305 *Good-quality Chinese antiques and furniture.*

Princess & Thepea, 10 Mount Faber Rd, Singapore 099199. Email: janne@princess-pea.com *Thai and Chinese silk furnishings and inventive cushions in brilliant hues.*

THAILAND

Asian Motifs 3rd floor, Gaysom Plaza, Ploenchit Rd, Pathumwan, Bangkok 10330. Email: carole@asianmotifs.com www.asianmotifs.com *High-quality celadon, ceramics and lacquerware made in Vietnam and Thailand specially for this establishment. Also hilltribe textiles.*

Cocoon Design 3rd floor, Gaysom Plaza, Ploenchit Rd, Pathumwan, Bangkok 10330. Email: cocoon@ksc.th.com *Thai and European designers combine to create funky Asian tableware and furnishings.*

Noble Art 3rd floor, Gaysom Plaza, Ploenchit Rd, Pathumwan, Bangkok 10330. Email: noble_art@hotmail.com *Sleek wooden vases in restrained designs; also home accessories.*

Jim Thompson 9 Surawong Rd, Bangkok 10500. Email: office@jimthompson.com *The classic source for Thai silks, home accessories and fashion.*

UK

Asian Art in London 32 Dover St, London W1S 4NE. Tel: + 44 (0)20 7499 2215. www.asianartinlondon.com *Provide extensive details of Asian art/furniture dealers in London.*

Barry Davies Oriental Art Ltd 1 Davies St, London W1K 3DB. Tel: + 44 (0)20 7408 0207 *Japanese antiques.*

Brandt Oriental Antiques 1st Floor, 29 New Bond St, London W1S 2RL. Tel: + 44(0)20 7499 8835 *China trade, Oriental accessories and Japanese metalwork.*

Cinnabar Dixies Barns, High Street, Ashwell, Hertfordshire SG7 5NS. Tel: + 44 (0)1462 743432 www.cinnabar.co.uk *Oriental furniture and decorative objects.*

Dragonfly Upper Norton Farm, Nr. Norton, Hampshire SO21 3QF. Tel: + 44 (0)1962 761616 www.wayforward.co.uk/dragonfly *Chinese and Indian furniture and textiles.*

Ebenezer Wildwood 58 Essex Rd, London N1 8LR. Tel: + 44 (0)20 7226 2294 www.ebenezerwildwood.co.uk *Antique and new furniture designs in exotic woods from China, Indonesia, Malaysia and Singapore.*

Forge Interiors South St, Rotherfield, Sussex TN6 3LN. Tel: + 44 (0)1892 853000 www.forgeinteriors.com *Antique Asian furniture and decorative items.*

General Trading Company 2 Symons St, Sloane Square, London SW3 2TJ. Tel: +44 (0)20 7730 0411 *East meets West – contemporary and traditional Oriental furniture, statues*

and decorative accessories. Catalogue available.

Gregg Baker Oriental Art 132 Kensington Church St, London W8 4BH. Tel: + 44 (0)20 7221 3533 *Japanese and Chinese works of art; specializes in paper screens and metalwork.*

Indigo 275 New Kings Rd, London SW6 4RD. Tel: + 44 (0)20 7384 3101 www.indigo-uk.com *Dealers and restorers of antique furniture and arts from India, China, Indonesia and Japan. Also shop in Bath, warehouse in Wiltshire.*

Kara Kara 2A Pond Place, South Kensington, London SW3 6QJ, UK. Tel: + 44 (0)20 7591 0891 *Unusual Japanese home accessories, including traditional teapots.*

Ki Design 594 King's Rd, London SW6 2DX. Tel: + 44 (0)20 7736 5999 *Oriental ceramics and furniture.*

Lombok 555 Kings Road, London SW6 2EB. Tel: + 44 (0)20 7736 0001 www.lombok.co.uk *Original furniture and accessories from Indonesia.*

Minh Mang 182 Battersea Park Rd, London SW11 4ND. Tel: + 44 (0)20 7498 3233 *Vietnamese silk and lacquerware.*

Nom 150 Walton Street, London SW3 2JJ. Tel/fax: + 44 (0)20 7584 4158 *Purist designs of Vietnamese lacquer, silver and ceramics.*

Emily Readett-Bailey Elmtree House, 54 Main Rd, Long Bennington, Lincolnshire NG23 5DJ. Tel: + 44 (0)1400 281563 Email: emily-readett-b@demon.co.uk *Bamboo, coconut-palm wood and mother-of-pearl home accessories made in Bali.*

Gordon Reece Gallery 16 Clifford St, London W1X 1RG. Tel: + 44 (0)20 7439 0007 Email: info@gordonreecegallery.co.uk *Wide selection of Japanese, Chinese and Central Asian furniture, rugs, artefacts and textiles.*

Revelloyd 124 Upper St, London N1 1QP. Tel: + 44 (0)20 7226 8501 *Oriental decorative accessories.*

Snap Dragon 247 Fulham Rd, London SW3 6HY. Tel: + 44 (0)20 7376 8889 *Oriental antiques.*

Soo San 598A Kings Rd, London SW6 2DX. Tel: + 44 (0)20 7731 2063 www.soosan.co.uk *Asian interiors and works of art; specializes in Chinese and Tibetan furniture, ceramics and Oriental decorative accessories.*

Spice Islander 305 Westbourne Grove, London W11 2QA. Tel: + 44 (0)20 7243 8140 www.spiceislander.co.uk *Indonesian home accessories.*

The Dragon & the Phoenix 24 East Street, South Molton, North Devon EX36 3DB. Tel: + 44 (0)1769 574104 www.dragonphoenix.co.uk *Antique Chinese furniture.*

Grace Wu Bruce 12a Balfour Mews, London W1K 2BJ. Tel: + 44 (0)20 7499 3750 Email: art@grace-wu-bruce.com *Acknowledged expert on and dealer in Chinese Ming furniture.*

Index